TEIKYO WESTMAR UNIV. LIBRARY W9-CDU-228

Women as Interpreters
of the Bible

Frontispiece:
"Diana Reading" from Christine de Pisan's *Epistre Othéa.*

Women as Interpreters of the Bible

Patricia Demers

41-1831

Paulist Press
New York/Mahwah, N.J.

ACKNOWLEDGMENTS

The Publisher gratefully acknowledges use of the following materials: a reprint of *Ave generosa* and its translation "Hymn to the Virgin" reprinted from St. Hildegard of Bingen: *Symphonia: A Critical Edition of the Symphonia armonie celestium revelationum*, edited and translated by Barbara Newman. Copyright © 1988 by Cornell University. Used by permission of the publisher, Cornell University Press; permission to use quotations from *Hildegard of Bingen's Scivias*, translated by Bruce Hozeski, © 1986 by Bear & Company, Inc. and from *Hildegard of Bingen's Book of Divine Works*, edited by Matthew Fox, OP, © 1987 by Bear & Company, Inc., has been granted by the publisher, Bear & Company, P.O. drawer 2860, Sante Fe, NM 87504-2860; a poem reprinted by permission of the publishers and the Trustees of Amherst College from *The Poems of Emily Dickinson*, Thomas H. Johnson, ed., Cambridge, Mass.; The Belknap Press of Harvard University Press, Copyright 1951, © 1955, 1979, 1983 by the President and Fellows of Harvard College; the illustration of Ecclesia from Wisse die Wege. *Scivias* by Hildegard von Bingen, Otto Muller Verlag Salzburg, 8.Aufl., 1987; two figures: the pagan statuette and the *sedes sapientiae* from Ilene Forsyth's *The Throne of Wisdom*, © 1972, Princeton University Press; the illustration from Christine de Pisan's Epistre Othéa from Bibliothèque Nationale, Paris; Kent Kraft's translation of Hildegard of Bingen's *Ave generosa*, *Vox Benedictina* 1 (1984), Peregrina Publishing Company, Toronto, Ontario, Canada.

Copyright © 1992 by Patricia Demers

All rights reserved. No part of this book may be reproduced or transmitted in any form or by any means, electronic or mechanical, including photocopying, recording, or by any information storage and retrieval system without permission in writing from the publisher.

Library of Congress Cataloging-in-Publication Data

Demers, Patricia, 1946–
    Women as interpreters of the Bible / Patricia Demers.
        p.   cm.
    Includes bibliographical references and index.
    ISBN 0-8091-3291-5 (pbk.)
    1. Bible—Criticism, interpretation, etc.—History.   2. Women
Biblical scholars.   I. Title.
BS500.D46   1991
220.6'082–dc20
                                                          91-38784
                                                          CIP

Published by Paulist Press
997 Macarthur Blvd.
Mahwah, N.J. 07430

Printed and bound in the United States of America

Contents

To my mother, Margaret, and in memory of
my father, Louis-Cyrille

Acknowledgements
I am deeply grateful to Father Terence Forestell, C.S.B., for attending the lectures in the first place, and then, for encouraging me to
consider publication. A colleague in Religious Studies, Francis
Landy, has been very patient with my halting attempts to transliter-
ate the Hebrew. Special thanks go to the graduate students—past
and present—who, in dramatizing the texts, made them come
alive for me as well as the audience: Elizabeth Hollis Berry, Joel
Cochrane, Bill Davies, Pam Farvolden, David Gay, Bev Matiko, and
Heather Zwicker.

Preface

> To see the good and the beautiful, and to have no
> strength to live it, is only to be Moses on the mountain of
> Nebo, with the land at your feet and no power to enter. It
> would be better not to see it.
> —Olive Schreiner, *The Story of an African Farm*

This study is an attempt to sketch and explain some of the
variety of women's accomplishments as interpretive readers of the
Bible. It began as a series of talks named in honor of our first
Chair, the Edmund Kemper Broadus lectures, which my Depart-
ment invited me to give on a topic of my choice. Though still a
neophyte in feminist hermeneutics, I felt both drawn in agreement
with most of its arguments and disposed to see current work in
light of women's earlier, mainly overlooked efforts.

Writing about interpretation can be as slippery and elusive as
the act of interpreting itself. When the focus is on the Judeo-
Christian scriptures as well as a gender-specific group of interpreters, it is critical for me to declare where I stand and what I hope to
accomplish. I hold interpretation to be much more than verbal
legerdemain or sophisms of equivocation. Concerned with explicating the quality, relation, and representation of being and grasping
the manifold substance of the text itself, interpretation, as a
construal of the text's sense, is an act of meaning. "Every act of
meaning is embedded in a context, and these contexts inexorably
change" (Meyer 24–5). This project is itself testimony to a continually changing context.

The title will, no doubt, strike some readers as an overdue
examination of forgotten women, and others as a curiously dated
rehearsal. I consider myself a feminist; however, I do admit that
the idea of thinking against the patriarchal tradition was neither

1

an available nor an espoused option for many of the women discussed in the following chapters. And so, first of all, I am not
attempting to color or shape the earlier writing to conform to
current feminist ideology. This assertion raises two issues: the importance of contextualization and the multiplicity of feminisms. At
present some theoreticians have inscribed difference as such a
hallmark of female discourse that it has become as imprisoning
and exclusive as the white, male power structure they are so vigor-
ously denouncing. A few have all but boxed themselves in to a
form of feminist essentialism. Aware that certain critics are prepared to dismiss this undertaking as a parade of commemorative
preservers and historians of masculine wisdom, who happened to
be women, I see the matter altogether differently. Since, with rare
exceptions, the writing of these women is so neglected, and since,
as a teacher of English, I lay no claim to being a theologian or a
philosopher, I have chosen to let the texts speak for themselves
and to unfold, as much as they can, their own contexts.

In stressing their words and limiting the context, I have not
tried to constrict or devalue the interplay between the individual
and the collective. Their links to one another are actually inescapable. While interpretation itself emerges from individual experience, the experience is a reflection of one's membership in a community or tradition. Furthermore, when sifting or, as some would
prefer, processing the links joining experience and interpretation,
we find ourselves also dealing with a whole cluster of intercon-
nected binaries: "language/ the extralinguistic; the word/ the utterance; sense/ meaning; denotation/ reference; . . . static/ revisable;
repetitive/ creative; mirroring/ mapping" (Jenkins 231). Since the
world of the biblical text these interpreters are addressing has
aspects which are cosmic, communitarian, historical, cultural, and
personal, it is necessary to be alert, as Paul Ricoeur reminds us, to
the " 'direction of meaning' of the word . . . its double power: that
of gathering together all the significations which issue from the
partial discourses, and that of opening up a horizon which escapes
from the closure of discourse" (Ricoeur 1975b, 28).

Perhaps because organized western religions, in general, deem
women's position and contribution more or less nugatory, women
interpreters have been especially drawn to speculate on the horizon
of possibilities rather than collecting the bouquets of received wisdom. Although some of the interpreters to be discussed were
branded heretical in their day, and others have clearly renounced
any affiliation with patriarchal religion, their combined, often dis-

cordant, voices affirm that investigating how, what, and why words mean is an essential inquiry. Not only because they are so little known, but also because their textual probings are so galvanizing, they can jolt us into a new understanding of John Donne's dictum, in the third Satire:

> In a strange way
> To stand inquiring right, is not to stray;
> To sleepe, or runne wrong, is. (lines 77–9)

The most energizing and determined of these interpreters would probably disagree with the conclusion of Olive Schreiner's heroine. Unlike her, they speak in a consciously utopian way, arguing that it is on account of the empowering possibilities they foresee that they write as inquiring interpreters.

Their inquiries have spread into many fields. I started this project with a very straightforward understanding of any conscious use or demonstration of familiarity with biblical narrative and dicta, in rhetoric fulfilling a persuasive, epideictic (demonstrative), or deliberative function, as a form of interpretation. I quickly became impressed with the variations women had worked on this all-purpose definition. Women's interpretive usage has produced dramas, hymns, prophetic treatises, meditations, diatribes, polemics, alphabets, allegories, verses, and tales, along with essays and studies exposing the centuries-old devaluation and suspicion of the female in patriarchal society. Although these forms have emerged from varying cultural milieux, women's work on biblical texts as illuminators, exegetes, polemicists, preceptors, theologians, and academics has always been far from abstraction. Practical in orientation and reformative in inspiration, their energetic works have been inducements to action; and predictably, too, reaction to them has ranged all the way from remorse to anger, from gratitude for instruction to belligerent dismissal. I hope readers will share some of my own excitement in listening to these distant and modern voices of women interpreters.

1

Women's Interpretive Work: Tradition and Difference

Indeed, she herself was so trained in Scripture interpretation that the Bible never left her holy hands. . . . Fulfilling the work of Martha, she began henceforth to imitate Mary, who was extolled in the Gospel as having chosen the good part.

—*The Life of Melania the Younger*

I have teaching within me, as it were the beginning of an ABC, whereby I may have some understanding of our Lord's meaning, for the mysteries of the revelation are hidden in it.

—Julian of Norwich, *Showings*

Believe me, Martha and Mary must join together in order to show hospitality to the Lord. . . . How would Mary, always seated at His feet, provide Him with food if her sister did not help her?

—Teresa of Avila, *The Interior Castle*

Views of Interpretation, the Bible, and Women's Interpreting

An interpreter's work is never really done. As cunning and shape-shifting as the messenger-god whose name supplies the root of the word describing the theories of interpretation known as hermeneutics, this work involves suppositions touching on perception and understanding, on concepts of history and language, and on the authority, rights, and duties claimed by the seeker of truth. Its questions, while ontological and epistemological, also invariably mirror the culture of the interpreter. A predictable combination of exegesis and eisegesis, reading out of and into the text, and of meaning and reference, the undertaking encourages advocacy argument. Interpretation, then, is never single, universal, and timeless, but always multiple, particular, and time-bound.

When, however, two complicating factors are blended in to the consideration of this already complex endeavor, the prospects of defining it simply and succinctly become more and more remote. When the text is the Bible and the interpreters are women, problematic issues abound. With an inherently religious text, whose theology and ethics have been the subject of constant, both affirmative and critical, examination, advocacy argument can run all the way from confessional, denominational, and normative explanations to secular and post-Christian denunciations. As well as reflecting historically conditioned concepts, some interpretive studies strive to reconcile reason and faith, while others pointedly resist or deny the distinction. Consider the multiplicity of views in our own culture concerning the Hebrew Tanakh and the Old and New Testaments. For many the issue of the interpretation of the Bible by either women or men is dead, non-existent, or irrelevant. Still others will find no viable, non-sexist paradigms at all in Judeo-Christian texts. The Bible is for some a literary but no longer normative document entailing insight into social differences; others see it as a series of "faith responses to concrete historical situations" (Fiorenza 1983, 33); for yet another group it provides a repository of inspired, inerrant proof texts to legitimize and monitor social practices. From the standpoint of "an academic . . . endeavor," those who try to make biblical narratives "models for their own behavior" are criticized because, in Mieke Bal's assessment, their "religious bias" with its "resulting idealistic view [and] moralistic isotopy of good and evil . . . spoils . . . the strong claim . . . about the social meaning of texts" (Bal 1988c, 139, 141). Her semiotic and narratological analysis operates from the outside, deliberately excising matters of faith and religion from the interpretation.

Other critics and interpreters, however, still write from the inside, for, as Ben Meyer observes, "the cost of discipleship is higher than the cost of scholarship" (208). I do not wish to impute any sort of garrison mentality to those who operate within a community of faith or a religious tradition of interpretation. As a matter of fact they have often expressed a bemused interest in secular, non-Christian, or post-Christian theorists who are seizing scripture back again as their own best exegetical proving ground.

Mary Ann Radzinowicz has succinctly itemized the features of biblical narrative which make it so attractive to "the currently constituted interpretive community . . . : (1) indeterminacy; (2) the canonical management of generic disunity; (3) the politics of reading
and the constitution of interpretive community; and (4) writing as
transgression or subversion" (79). Robert Morgan and John Barton, moreover, enumerate the difficulties and prospects of writing
from the inside. They position the task of biblical interpretation in
the milieu of post-structuralist theory, where humanist assumptions are challenged and textual meaning, if not subverted, is radically indeterminate. Concentrating on the "paradoxical" participation of Christian theologians in this struggle, Morgan and Barton
describe them as having "something distinctive to say," but "sus-
pected of sound and fury signifying nothing." This is how they
outline the theologians' double bind:

> The religious community can only offer, never impose.
> What it offers can be made visible only in the lives of its
> members. This community life is sustained in part by con-
> structive theological interpretation of its scriptures. These
> are designed in the first place for those who share a set of
> assumptions which are no longer self-evident, but they also
> aim to persuade, and their assumptions are open to correc-
> tion or development in the light of new knowledge or
> moral insight. (259)

Ironically, though, the informed sweep of Morgan and Barton's survey in *Biblical Interpretation* is remarkable for the slight
detail devoted to the transforming energies of feminist theology
and hermeneutics. A decade or two earlier, such omission or silence would have constituted an accurate account of the way things
were. Despite the assurances of the often-quoted passage in Galatians (3:28), interpretation of the Bible has made much of the
distinction between male and female. *The Interpreter's Bible,* the
twelve-volume project spanning the 1950s, has a lone woman—
Louise Pettibone Smith writing on the Book of Ruth—among its
124 contributors. *The Jerome Biblical Commentary's* slightly higher
average consists of two out of fifty contributors. *The Interpreter's
Dictionary of the Bible,* in general, provides more representation—
with seven women contributing to the initial four volumes and
eighteen (out of 272) to the 1976 Supplement. While the Editor's
Preface to the 1962 volumes cited such "new knowledge" as

" 'higher criticism,' " "form criticism" and the archaeological discoveries at Qumran and Jericho as helping to teach "that only
Bible verities about the nature of man can withstand history's stern
tests" (xviii), the Supplement's editor drew attention to new articles
on topics like "the status of women" as proof of the Bible's "ability
to speak to changing concerns of society" and the need to understand "the men and women of the Bible . . . in the light of their
contemporary cultures" (xx). The point is not to establish a mere
arithmetical criterion, not to light on any mention of "women" as
having a talismanic significance, but to underscore the differences
and revisions which feminism has instigated.

During the last two decades the scholarship of feminist theologians, exegetes, and hermeneuts—among them, Carol Christ,
Mary Daly, Elisabeth Schüssler Fiorenza, Eleanor McLaughlin,
Rosemary Radford Ruether, Letty Russell, and Phyllis Trible—has
questioned the whole foundation on which earlier and male-
dominated interpretations have rested. Yet the work of the last
fifteen or twenty years is as much a reflection of specific times and
personalities as the deeds of the ancient Israelites whom it studies.
Scholars today work in an intellectual and secular climate that
tends to value skepticism over tradition. Unlike the biblical women
on whom their writing often focuses, scholars rarely speak on be-
half of a community of faith. Even when they do, they clearly
challenge hierarchical, exclusive readings of scripture to effect
new understandings of experience and tradition, and a fundamental redefinition of order in human society. In contradistinction to
the prescription of the 1943 papal encyclical *Divino afflante Spiritu*
("On the Outpouring of the Spirit," also known as "On Biblical
Studies") that "commentators must have as their chief object to
show what is the theological doctrine touching faith and morals of
each book and text" (n. 24), these scholars are most interested in
exploring and clarifying perceptions of divinity and humanness
and of existence and belief, as they continue to influence our lives.
Approaching the Bible from such diverse vantage points as comparative anthropology, Near Eastern history, and narratological
theory, their writing suggests various ways of parsing the language
of literature and, for some, the language of faith.

The Evolving Art of Interpretation

When compounding such particulars as interpretation, biblical interpretation, and women's biblical interpretation, one of the

greatest temptations, it seems to me, is to accept the present as the norm, to adopt the fallacy which Margaret Alexiou has labeled "paronto-centrism" (Bal 1988c, 138). Since I was attracted to this project in the first place by the idea of examining the differing forms women's interpretive work has assumed and the reasons for either its notoriety or neglect, it appears both logical and consistent to accord the same treatment to all the constitutive elements of the undertaking. I propose the following thumbnail sketches not as exhaustive histories or charts of evolutionary progress, but as an indication of the heritage which contemporary work consciously draws on or negates.

The science or art of interpretation always involves questions of being and time as well as concepts of human capacity, culture, and history. Although Aristotle's treatise on interpretation, *Peri Hermeneias*, was available in a Latin translation, *De Interpretatione*, by 1128, it was not until the time of the German enlightenment that writers like Johann Martin Chladenius disagreed openly with the Aristotelian understanding of interpretation as essentially a grammatical logic which set out to define nouns, verbs, and statements. Aristotle's concern to delimit the sphere of affirmation and to demonstrate that what is affirmed is not automatically true prompted him to concentrate on the distinction between possibility and necessity. As he reasoned,

> What is, necessarily is, when it is; and what is not, necessarily is not, when it is not. But not everything that is, necessarily is; and not everything that is not, necessarily is not. (9a. 23–25)

In his commentary on the *Peri Hermeneias* Thomas Aquinas laid more stress on enunciation than interpretation for, as he argued through a citation from Boethius, Aristotle's work really concerns "significant vocal sound—whether complex or incomplex—which signifies something by itself" (Book I, n.3).

Interpretation, of course, extends to more than grammatical understanding and affirmative enunciations; it comprises a whole spectrum of means of making sense of seen and unseen, experienced and described, events. In spite of his protests that interpretations, in the sense of oneirocriticism, "belong to God" (Gen 40:8), Joseph nonetheless proceeds to explain the dreams of the pharaoh's imprisoned butler and baker, to the benefit of one and death of the other. But the divination of visions, as practiced by Joseph and

Daniel, is but one of many possible forms of interpretation. To expound or take in a specified manner favorably or adversely is the denotation of Pico della Mirandola's praise of man, in his *Oration on the Dignity of Man,* as the "interpreter of nature," which Pico considers "the interval between fixed eternity and fleeting time."[1] Francis Bacon conveys a similar idea in his self-description as "a true priest of the sense . . . and a not unskilful interpreter of its oracles" ("The Plan of the Work," *The Great Instauration*). Baconian induction also accounts for the hierarchy of Solomon's House, in *The New Atlantis,* where the highest functionaries who "raise the former discoveries by experiments into greater observations, axioms and aphorisms" are called Interpreters of Nature. Interpreters may expound, elucidate, explain, perform, and translate. Of particular interest in view of the roles of elucidation and translation is George Puttenham's definition, in *The Arte of English Poesie,* of the rhetorical figure of the Interpreter, which he prefers to call the figure of store that beautifies by enlarging and describing one thing by a host of others:

> The Greekes call it Sinonimia; . . . the Latines . . . called it by a name of event, for (said they) many words of one nature and sence, one of them doth expound another. And therefore they called this figure the *Interpreter.* (214)

The various sorts of analogues or comparisons which the interpreter could adduce preoccupied German theorists of hermeneutics several generations later. While Chladenius was confident of arriving at complete and unambiguous understanding by comparing the observer's words with what could be gleaned from other sources, Friedrich Schleiermacher, the true initiator of hermeneutics as an academic discipline, viewed the endeavor as altogether more complex and changeable, rooted in the intricate variables of language usage and individual character. During the first two decades of the nineteenth century Schleiermacher was insisting that historical sources be examined for the claim they still hold on life and that hermeneutics combine both universal-objective factors (what he called "grammatical interpretation") and particular-subjective (the "technical or psychological interpretation") factors. Grammatical interpretation, as he explained it, comprises a wide range of linguistic speculation:

> The distinctive nature of a language is the specific modification of its view of the world. . . . The individuality of a

> people's language is connected to the individuality mani-
> fest in all its other common activities. . . . In grammatical
> interpretation to understand a language completely would
> be to understand its center. (163)

Psychological interpretation is a necessary partner in the hermeneutic activity because it emphasizes the ultimately unlimited connections between style and psyche:

> Character, the individual nature of an author, is a specific
> modification of the ability to think. . . . The individuality
> manifest in a person's way of combining and presenting
> thoughts is connected with every other expression of his
> individuality. . . . In technical interpretation style is under-
> stood only by a fully complete knowledge of an author's
> character. (164)

Although many theories that were largely complementary to
and derivative of Schleiermacher's work, such as Wilhelm von
Humboldt's understanding of history in concrete, individual phenomena and the philological tacks of Johann Droysen and August
Boeckh, followed, the hermeneutic theorist who moved the whole
discipline closer to an examination of lived experience and an
existential principle was Wilhelm Dilthey. Locating interpretation
in the interaction between other people's "life-expressions" and
our own experience and self-understanding, Dilthey concluded in
favor of the subjectivity and lack of logical formula in understanding, which "contains something irrational because life is irrational."[2] The connections between meaning, activity, and experience
dominated Edmund Husserl's investigations in phenomenology
along with Martin Heidegger's concept of a basic state of Being-in-
the-world. One of the most polemical extensions of the Heidegger-
ian analysis of existence in relation to being emerged in Rudolf
Bultmann's inquiry into the theology of meaning; by way of the
demythologizing process undertaken through *Sachkritik* (material
or objective criticism) in *Jesus Christ and Mythology,* he attempted to
separate the essence from the particular objectification, in the conviction that the meaning of scripture discloses itself anew and
afresh in every future. While Bultmann melded philosophy and
theology, Paul Ricoeur sought to recover a concept of revelation as
a hermeneutics of testimony involving the "creative imagination of
the possible" (Ricoeur 1980, 161), which need not stand in opposi-

tion to reason. In addition, quite unlike the stance later adopted by Bal about the spoiling religious bias, Ricoeur welcomes the hermeneutics of testimony as a defensible academic pursuit, even though it will never correspond to the scientific ideal of absolute knowledge and even though the thetic judgments of testimony will never constitute unarguable proof.

Increasingly the issues of the bases of authority and the feasibility of objectivity engross critics' attention. In an era of meta-interpretive analysis the central questions involve whom to trust and how to assess. As part of his contribution to a discussion of the politics of interpretation Hayden White applauds the unfashionable politics of vision, which grounds its eschatological hope for a rule of the saints and a perfected society on "an apperception of history's meaninglessness . . . as a 'spectacle' of 'confusion,' 'uncertainty,' and 'moral anarchy' " (128).[3] Rather than picturing history reverentially and objectively as a window through which to see the past, White prefers to apprehend it as "a wall that must be broken through if the 'terror of history' is to be directly confronted and the fear it induces dispelled" (137). Two recent studies, which appear to me to fulfill this very criterion, examine the status and roles of women in ancient and early post-biblical Israel. Although the active role of women in such a household-oriented society as ancient Israel was not a matter of public written record, Carol Meyers applies the insights of social anthropology, in *Discovering Eve*, to argue convincingly that the woman was "no less powerful than her male counterpart" (181). By contrast, the dichotomizing of gender attributes that is so evident in post-biblical documents, especially the Mishnah, the legal rules compiled by sages in second century Roman Palestine, is the subject of Judith Romney Wegner's investigation, *Chattel or Person?;* with precision she deconstructs the motives which generally subordinated women to men's needs in mishnaic society and, on rare occasions, allowed women a degree of personhood. Though Hazard Adams' concern is more with literary than jurisprudential texts, he is aware of the operation of comparable power criteria in the establishment of any canonical literature; to provide for renewal and a responsive understanding of power relations Adams encourages the role of the antithetical, by which "every discourse striving for power must be opposed by a discourse struggling against its own tendency to invoke power criteria" (753). However, as any awareness of the stormy history of biblical interpretation, in particular, leads the reader to infer, such antithetical discourse is easier to theorize about than to practice.

Theories of Biblical Interpretation

When the text under consideration is not just the major storehouse of symbol and allusion for the English literary tradition but the privileged, authoritative, and visionary text for many communities of faith, it is difficult—if not impossible—to follow Benjamin Jowett's directive to the letter: to "read the Bible like any other book," disregarding "all the after-thoughts of theology" (338). For it is precisely the theological after-thoughts and presuppositions of lay and ordained, secular and religious, readers that have sparked the crises and developments in biblical interpretation.

In the earliest treatises on the subject church fathers and exegetes were quick to seize on the charismatic convert Paul as the model rhetor and pedagogue for their purposes. How fitting it was that he had actually been called "Mercurius" (Acts 14:12). The interpreter was essentially a persuasive, informed teacher, as effective at engaging a listener as at uncovering hidden riches. A favorite example was Philip's role as guide and preacher in explaining the scripture to the Ethiopian eunuch (Acts 8:27–40); Philip's being sent by the angel of the Lord is as noteworthy as his success, since this commission highlighted the special divine sanction of interpretive activity.

Examining some of the diverse metaphors used in these early works to describe the word which the interpreter attempts to explain discloses the solemnity and close-to-sacramental importance of interpretation. As Clement of Alexandria figured the transformative, kerygmatic energies of scripture in *The Protreptikos,* the Logos is salvific and constructive:

> The Word of truth, the Word of incorruption, that regenerates man by bringing him back to the truth—the goad that urges to salvation—He who expels destruction and pursues death—He who builds up the temple of God in men. (Chapter XI)

Many of Clement's contemporaries and successors continued to marvel at the unfolding truth of the sacred texts. Origen devoted his *First Principles* to reverence for and understanding of scripture as inspired writing which, he admitted, contains many impossible, apparently irrational statements. An example of strict Origenist logic is his comment on the injunction to turn the left cheek to an assailant (Mt 5:39), who would have had to have been a left-handed aggressor in order to avoid a mere repetition of injury, "since anyone who struck with the right hand would hit the left cheek" (Book IV, chapter 3). Not content with such syntactical exactitude, Origen points the reader to inner spiritual meaning: "the aim of the Holy Scripture is that we should understand that there have been woven into the visible narrative truths that, if pondered and understood inwardly, bring forth a law useful to men and worthy of God." Although Jerome later joined in a condemnation of Origen, this famous translator was also an apologist for Christian interpretation; moreover, Jerome's metaphors, describing the process of translating the sense and not the word, echo Origen's images. In his preface to the Vulgate version of the Old Testament Jerome termed the Hebrew Bible "the alphabet of the doctrine of God" (489), and in the service of this doctrine he maintained a perfectionist's passion for accuracy; he pictured himself as both a master vintner, whose product "has been drawn straight from the press, and stored in a clean jar, and has thus preserved its own flavour," and as an astute farmer, who "cross-plough[s] the land which has already been broken up, and, by means of the transverse furrows . . . root[s] out the thorns which are beginning to spring again" (Prefaces to Proverbs, Ecclesiastes, the Song of Songs and the Psalms, VI: 492, 494). John Chrysostom's treatise *On the Priesthood* renews emphasis on the holy duty involved in hermeneutics, by citing the work of Paul in Thessalonica, Corinth, Ephesus, and Rome, spending "whole nights and days in interpreting the Scriptures," as an exhortation to priests, for the sake of their flock, "to be experienced in disputations of this kind" (Book IV). Augustine's *On Christian Doctrine* is a repository of orthodox opinion about the singular importance of biblical interpretation, whose purpose is "both to teach what is right and to refute what is wrong" (Book IV, Chapter 4). In "ascertaining the proper meaning and . . . making known the meaning when it is ascertained," the interpreter is "like one who teaches reading, that is, shows others how to read for themselves" (Book I, chapter 1). Yet in Augustine's concern for pedagogic thoroughness he also allows for a diversity of interpretations which may "touch at some point" (Book II, chapter 12).

    The results, however, ended up being more than contiguous.

Early medieval commentaries tended to be so congruent and uniform that, as Robert McNally concludes, "no other age understood Holy Scripture as poorly as this one" (79). McNally cites commentators' preoccupation with spiritual at the expense of literal meanings and their "ultraconservatism" (63) as contributing factors. In tracing the monastic "ascent to God," he speculates that the medieval Bible became a combination of *theoria* and *actualis,* giving "life to work and light to prayer" (80). Although not one woman is included in McNally's catalogue of commentators, my study intends to pursue the applicability of this blending to the mainly overlooked work of religious women.

The distinct academic function of teaching and interpreting the Bible was usually designated, as Beryl Smalley explains in her monumental work on biblical studies in northwestern Europe to 1300, by the title *magister sacre pagine* (316); in contrasting the exegeses of Paris and Byzantium, she notes that in the east studies in the New Testament predominated, while in the west medieval scholarship favored the study of Hebrew, with the rabbi appealing "as a kind of telephone to the Old Testament" (362). For the Latin scholar, according to Smalley, Hebrew captured "his emotions, his philosophy, and his sense of history" (363). It is only in a fifteenth century list that she uncovers the title of the Byzantine master, assigned to teach the Old Testament, as " 'rhetor interpreter of Scripture' " (361). Female writers and interpreters, however, are scarcely mentioned in *The Study of the Bible in the Middle Ages.* They usually operated within the confines of convents, abbeys, beguine communities, or anchorholds. Their work was often published well after their deaths. And, in contrast to scholastic pedagogy, the tradition of Hildegard of Bingen, Mechthild of Magdeburg, Hadewijch of Brabant, and Julian of Norwich is strongly affective and mystical.

In the field of biblical interpretation the claims of the opposition, as distinct from the minority, have always been audible and influential. Just as the severest challenge to post-reformation Catholic and Protestant traditions was the natural religion and anti-supernatural deism of the enlightenment, the biggest impediment to either ecclesiastical or independent interpretation today seems to be the general disregard for the activity in our post-Christian pluralistic culture. However gargantuan and heterodox the field of biblical criticism may seem to students of religion and literature, it quickly shrinks to insignificance when compared to commentaries on other cultural pursuits and entertainments. For one vocal movement, though, biblical criticism is of clearly-felt influence and importance. Feminism, which is proving relentless in its exposure of androcentric bias and patriarchal privilege, is the major reformative impulse evident in interpretive studies. Whether impatiently scolding or painstakingly deconstructing these embedded assumptions, or whether rereading to reclaim heroines and valorize liberating, egalitarian paradigms, feminist hermeneutics offers a key vital sign in contemporary biblical interpretation.

Biblical Women as Possible Models

The work itself is reminiscent of the audacity of some famous and not-so-famous biblical women, even though the suggestion of biblical models is an anachronistic misinterpretation for certain readers. The strength of feminist exegesis is in many ways like that of the prophetess Huldah. When Hilkiah, Ahikam, Achbor, Shaphan, and Asahiah consulted and "communed with her" in the college in Jerusalem where she dwelt, Huldah related to them this message:

> Thus says the Lord, the God of Israel: "Tell the man who sent you to me, Thus says the Lord, Behold, I will bring evil upon this place and upon its inhabitants, all the words of the book which the king of Judah has read. Because they have forsaken me and have burned incense to other gods, that they might provoke me to anger with all the work of their hands, therefore my wrath will be kindled against this place, and it will not be quenched. But as to the king of Judah, who sent you to inquire of the Lord, thus shall you say to him, Thus says the Lord, the God of Israel: Regarding the words which you have heard, because your heart was penitent, and you humbled yourself before the Lord, when you heard how I spoke against this place, and against its inhabitants, that they should become a desolation and a curse, and you have rent your clothes and wept before me, I also have heard you, says the Lord. Therefore, behold . . . you shall be gathered to your grave in peace, and your eyes shall not see all the evil which I will bring upon this place." (2 Kgs 22:15–20)

Excepting Josiah on account of his piety, her words are really a summary of what has happened. While her prophetic voice as a combination of anger and reassurance—a mixture which parallels some of the themes in feminist theology—is not greatly different in tone from that of the male prophets, it is significant that her name and predictions of disaster attending an incorrect understanding of the law are so little known; feminist readers are not content to dismiss Huldah simply as a relayer of words second-hand, a mere stipended speaker or *porte parole*.

In other instances in the Hebrew Bible not only do female prophecy, leadership, and bravery convey the importance of these women in ways which pointedly shame men, but the women's questioning or criticism of authority promotes their kinship with today's exegetes and critics. As prophetess and judge Deborah is accustomed to "the people of Israel com[ing] up to her for judgment" (Jgs 4:5); her song makes clear the inseparability of poetry and prophecy, for "she offers . . . an explanation of what it means to judge: to pronounce the right word in a given situation, to establish order in the chaos by means of the right word" (Bal 1988b, 57). This "mother in Israel" (Jgs 5:7) summons Barak to fight the Canaanites under Sisera and even agrees to accompany him to the battle, during which another woman, Jael "of tent-dwelling women most blessed" (Jgs 5:24), kills the oppressor. "So too the mention of Noadiah (Neh 6:14) suggests that there were probably more women acting as prophets in ancient Israel than Miriam, Deborah, and Huldah" (Adler 97). The ignominy of being defeated by a woman is clear in Abimelech's order to his armor-bearer, after an unnamed woman of Thebez has hurled a millstone at Abimelech's head: "Draw your sword and kill me, lest men say of me, 'A woman killed him' " (Jgs 9:54). Equally anonymous and crucial is the woman of Tekoa, whose wisdom prompts the reversal of a ruler's decision; it is a multi-faceted virtue, consisting of her ability to relay the story Joab had told her to David, her honesty in admitting its source to the king, and her poetic justification of the need to forgive Absalom: "We must all die, we are like water spilt on the ground, which cannot be gathered up again; but God will not take away the life of him who devises means not to keep his banished one an outcast" (2 Sam 14:14). In a male-centered society the counsel of the wise woman of Abel (2 Sam 20:16–22) is also heeded. Esther's decision to appear before King Ahasuerus, when she had not been called and "though it is against the law" (Est 4:16), shows that her real beauty lies in this spirited defense of her people.

Feminist Hermeneutics

Feminist studies have never lacked spirit. Mary Daly's *Beyond God the Father* is one of the first blasts of the trumpet against the monstrous regiment of men; by distancing herself from "kerygmatic theology" (7), she exposes "the deep problem of human becoming in women" (19), when the prevailing assumption is "that if God is male, then the male is God" (19). Women are, for Daly, "aliens" (28) in the terrain of biblical language. More ferocious and anti-theological is her indictment of the "Christian and Postchristian myth" in *Gyn/Ecology: The Metaethics of Radical Feminism.* Dichotomous, contorted, adversarial, and, for some of the attacked patriarchs, blasphemous, her writing constantly criticizes "religious reduction of real, multidimensional presence" (79), and opposes real and apparent triviality:

In the land of the Fathers, women are trivial, concerned with trivia, deserving to be trivialized. In the Prehistoric Background of Hags, the time/space of Trivia, women are free to find the cosmic triviality of our own complex creative power. (79)

Punning and turning in her own linguistic gyre, Daly concludes with this manifesto:

In the beginning was not the word. In the beginning is the hearing. Spinsters spin deeper into the listening deep. Spinning is celebration/cerebration. Spinsters spin all ways, always. Gyn/Ecology is Un-Creation; Gyn/Ecology is Creation. (424)

More consistently logical are the arguments of Rosemary Ruether and Elisabeth Fiorenza about the necessary combination of criticism and nurturance in the prophet's role. Maintaining that "human experience is both the starting point and the ending point of the circle of interpretation," Ruether insists that "the Bible can be appropriated as a source of liberating paradigms only if it can be seen that there is a correlation between the feminist critical principle and that critical principle by which biblical thought critiques itself and renews its vision as the authentic Word of God over against corrupting and sinful deformations" (Ruether 1985, 111, 117). For Fiorenza religion is not a sacred canopy protecting the status quo either. She grounds her "new scholarly paradigm of biblical interpretation" in the "experience of women, of women-church (*ekklesia gynaikon*)," suggesting that this process will transform "our metaphor of Scripture as 'tablets of stone' on which the unchanging word of God is engraved for all times into the image of bread that nurtures, sustains, and energizes women as people of God in our struggle against injustice and oppression" (Fiorenza 1984, x, xiv). Not all hermeneutic studies cherish the hope of transforming from within. Since its inception in 1985 the *Journal of Feminist Studies in Religion* regularly explores theological alternatives. Moreover, the editor of the *Semeia* (1983) issue devoted to "The Bible and Feminist Hermeneutics," Mary Ann Tolbert, remains dissatisfied with feminist biblical hermeneutics, wondering how long feminists can be pacified "with the discovery of the occasional or exceptional in a patriarchal religion"; for Tolbert the encounter with God "as enemy and friend, as tormentor and savior" (126), is the paradoxical challenge of this interpretive work.

For other readers such theological suppositions are not only anachronistic, but they preclude or prevent any radical critique. These readers consider it imperative to view the women in the Hebrew texts against the larger patrilineal and patriarchal background of their culture. Excluded from the census (Num 26), executed on the mere suspicion of adultery (Num 5:11–30), and labeled unclean for fourteen days after the birth of a female child as opposed to the seven day period following the birth of a male (Lev 12), the woman was definitely judged and defined by men. In her extended essay on abjection Julia Kristeva examines the dietary prohibitions and various temple practices related in the law as part of a "radical separating process . . . an attempt to keep a being who speaks to his God separated from the fecund mother" (100). If purity is conformity to an established taxonomy and impurity, "that which unsettles it, establishes intermixture and disorder" (98), then, Kristeva concludes, Judaism's prohibitions are "a matter of separating oneself from the phantasmatic power of the mother, that archaic Mother Goddess who actually haunted the imagination of a nation at war with the surrounding polytheism" (100). In addition to being separate, as Phyllis Trible demonstrates in her second book, *Texts of Terror*, women were often victimized; by retelling the stories of Hagar, David's daughter Tamar, the unnamed concubine at the close of the book of Judges, and Jephthah's daughter, she catalogues the strategies which silenced and marginalized women. The exceptions are either foreigners, like the Queen of Sheba and Ruth, or idol worshipers, like Jezebel and Delilah, or anonymous characters, like the wise women of David's reign, or mysteriously undeveloped figures, like Huldah and Noadiah. Mieke Bal's *Lethal Love* exposes the ways in which and speculates about the reason why "the female subject has been repressed or made guilty of all that did not fit" (5) in five biblical love stories: David and Bathsheba, Samson and Delilah, Ruth and Boaz, Judah and Tamar, and Adam and Eve. By presenting a semiotics of reading, she reveals the insecurity in patriarchal heroism, especially in the sexual fears of David, Samson, and Judah. Delilah and Tamar are for Bal psychoanalysts, teaching men insight into their "paralyzing neuroses" (102). Through politicizing theoretical terms *Lethal Love* explores a vein of feminist analysis different from that in *Texts of Terror*. Bal is interested in the Bible not as a Christian feminist resource or a sexist manifesto, but as an influential cultural, mythical, and literary document. She bases a more recent study, *Murder and Difference,* on the beliefs that "the activity of interpretation extends the limits of the discipline itself" and that "hermeneutics and interdisciplinarity go hand in hand" (3). As Bal argues, the textual object is always dynamic, unstable, elusive; sifting for meaning involves more than mere analysis: "to analyse how others attribute meaning is to interpret" (135). Examining the narrative of Sisera's death from the points of view of historical, theological, anthropological, and literary codes, she reserves the most startling observations for the codes of thematics and gender. Jael's act becomes one of "the few experiences this woman has by virtue of her own power: to mate, to give birth, and, now, to murder" (131). In Bal's assessment "killing assumes the form of inverted sexual intercourse, of false childbirth."

Inquiring into the ideological implications of biblical texts has led women to formulate various reunions of secular and religious critical traditions. In *Is God the Only Reliable Father?* Diane Tennis compares the images of God as Father with contemporary, often-absent fathers to support her argument that a "helpful theological task is to transform parent language for God [through] using mother language" (34). By showing how Jesus' parables and life-style offered "a radical challenge to patriarchy" (47), Sandra Schneiders promotes exegesis of the female aspects of the divine as a way of "healing the patriarchal imagination" (69). This exegetical emphasis places her *Women and the Word* in the tradition of such studies as Phyllis Trible's *God and the Rhetoric of Sexuality* (1978), Joan Engelsman's *The Feminine Dimension of the Divine* (1979), Sallie McFague's *Metaphorical Theology* (1982) and *Models of God* (1987), and Virginia Mollenkott's *The Divine Feminine* (1983). In *Searching for Lost Coins,* however, Ann Loades cautions against euphoria about the prospect of "using parental language for God, when we already know that it can be such a barrier to religious belief, depending on how the whole package is expressed and lived" (98). She causes us to recollect that submerged or disguised hatred of the father can surface in retaliation against the mother.

Another complementary and strong influence in current scholarship is the reexamination of women's roles and attributes, as glimpsed in ancient reliquiae, rituals, and texts, with the idea, as Margaret Miles put it, "that the area of intersection of religion and culture provides a fruitful nexus for exploring women's lives" (2). At times, though, conclusions differ markedly. Both Elaine Pagels, in *The Gnostic Gospels,* and Pheme Perkins, in *The Gnostic Dialogue,* for example, comment on the gnostic text, the Gospel of Mary, in which Mary explains her revelation about the savior to the amazement and initial ridicule of some of the disciples. Pagels seizes on this incident and the disciples' eventual acceptance of Mary's teaching to distinguish the gnostic "principle of equality between men and women" which was often adopted in "the social and political structures of their communities" (79) from the outlook of orthodox Christians who "retaliated" with an exclusively male theology and hierarchy. Examining the same text, Perkins does characterize Mary as "the initiator of the Gnostic tradition of interpreting the sayings of the Lord" (136). By contrast, however, Perkins stresses that anti-feminism was "a common presupposition of ancient ascetic writings"; her explanation of Mary's prominence as an interpreter relies on an understanding of this exceptional woman's social milieu; "Mary is a hero here not because of an extraordinary role played by women in Gnostic communities, but because she is a figure closely associated with Jesus to whom esoteric tradition may be attached" (136). Pagels' more recent book, *Adam, Eve and the Serpent,* compares Augustine and John Chrysostom; she lays the blame squarely on the bishop of Hippo for introducing opinions which have bedeviled and distorted interpretation over the centuries: a punitive notion of sexuality, an anti-naturalistic view of nature, and a sense of individual guilt for original sin. Just as texts can be interpreted differently and even tendentiously, symbols and figures expressing pre-patriarchal values can change to meet the needs of successive cultures. In *The Goddess Obscured* Pamela Berger traces the evolution of the figure of the protectress of grain and sowing, from a mother goddess to a saint, as a specific illustration of the point that "in each era people interpret anew the original revelatory paradigms of their faith" (146).

The Continuing Tradition of
Women's Interpretive Work

My aim in this study is a further reflection of change and continuity. While it is true that we have not seen anything like contemporary feminist studies before, their characteristic energy and reformative impulse have appeared in earlier stages and iterations. I propose to locate contemporary feminist biblical scholarship, and its alternate readings, suggested subtexts, and radical revisions, both in our cultural setting and within the continuous western tradition of women as interpreters of the Bible, which conventional statistics might seem to deny. Such an undertaking, I trust, will be neither narrow nor isolationist.

Since the accomplishments of medieval visionaries, renaissance reformers, and moral preceptors, who drew on and enlarged scriptural texts, have gone largely unnoticed until recently, it becomes even more important to integrate their work with the voices of contemporary women. Because interpretive work and religious conviction often formed the basis of political action, it seems both prudent and illuminating, for instance, to study the lives and writings of such early mothers of the church as Macrina, Paula, and Melania, such medieval saints as Lioba and Catherine of Siena, Marie Dentière's defense of women's rights to interpret the scriptures, which she composed as a letter to the queen of Navarre and published under her own name, and the account of the trial of the Protestant martyr, Anne Askew, burned as a heretic at Smithfield, after daring to interpret the Bible and refusing to recant in the face of Romish inquisitors. The links joining scripture interpretation to critical self-awareness and social responsibility are one of the salient features of women's work, as in Angelina Grimké's "Appeal to the Christian Women of the South" in the *Anti-Slavery Examiner* (1836), Matilda Joslyn Gage's contributions to the *History of Women Suffrage* (1881), and Elizabeth Cady Stanton's commentary in *The Woman's Bible* (1895). Women's interpretive work can be spoken of as a hermeneutic of being, in which knowing and doing are deeply and intricately related.

Initially some of the tonal mixtures of their voices may sound unharmonic. This apparent discord, attributable to differences in world view and degrees of religious and academic self-conscious-

ness, may yield a certain and special harmony. The intense purposiveness of the female interpretive tradition—its zeal and poise,
directness and sophistication—was what attracted me to this study
in the first place; uncovering the associations linking women's
work over a span of centuries has been for me a series of real
events and awakenings, which I hope the reader will share.

The mingling of contemporary, historical, and legendary figures in the spirit of reading anew and afresh, which this interpretive tradition encourages, continues to remind me of Christine de
Pisan's *Book of the City of Ladies.* The Roman "goddess" Carmentis,
on whose gifts of eloquence, inspiration, and prophecy Christine
lavishes considerable attention, has become for me a model or an
emblem of women's interpretive work. Inventing "her own letters,
which were completely different from those of other nations,"
Carmentis establishes the Latin alphabet, for as "it seemed to
her . . . it would not be right for the Romans to use the strange and
inferior letters and characters of another country" (72). That a
woman, in Christine's account, provides this fundamental tool of
literacy as well as introduction to the mystery of language supplies
a tidy analogy, I think, to the centuries-old work of women interpreters, who offer a distinctive initiation to the language and mystery of the Bible.

The connections between the Bible and society highlighted in
the tradition of women's interpretive work also help to explain the
links between Christine de Pisan's first published work, *Epistre
Othéa,* (see frontispiece) and the following chapters. This epistolary
political allegory, addressed from the goddess (o-thea) of wisdom to
the Trojan hero Hector, has many levels of possible meanings; Christine as Othéa urges practical political moderation on her knightly
subject, who could be Louis of Orléans, the mad king Charles VI,
the Duc de Berry, the queen Isabeau of Bavaria, or the dauphin
Louis of Guyenne. This well-read and well-informed widow was
taken seriously in the male world of political commentary; she herself supervised the production of the 101 illuminations accompanying the second and third manuscript versions of her work, which
was translated from French to English by Stephen Scrope as early as
the middle of the fifteenth century. The illumination of Diana Reading does, I hope, form a visual introduction to this study for a
variety of reasons. It is not the best-known illumination from Christine de Pisan's works, just as women's accomplishments as interpreters of the Bible are not readily identified. It depicts a community of
women absorbed in books and heeding the words of a celestial

female, forecasting the efforts of feminist exegetes to reclaim the
biblical imagery of the feminine. Christine, who described herself at
the time of her widowhood as transformed, "vrays homme fus
devenu" (*Le Livre de la Mutacion de Fortune,* line 1361), wastes no time
and sees no heresy in applying a biblical reading to this mythical
depiction and even making the "Lady Dyane" into God; as Scrope's
translation renders the correspondence,

> And for to bryng to mynde the Articles of Feyth to owre
> purpose, wythowte the which a good spirit may lytell
> avayle, ffor Dyane we shall take God of Heven, the which
> is withowte ony spotte off unclen love, to whome a thyng
> foulede with synne may not be agreable. (37)

Echoes of Huldah and Noadiah reverberate in fifteenth century
Paris.

The chapters to follow will examine various kinds of echoes
and silences, reverberations and shouts, which, as the epigraphs
imply, may be simultaneously affective and practical. The lyrical
self-confidence of medieval mystics, most of whom were members
of religious orders, characterize the devotional, instructive, and
theatrical uses to which they put their intimate knowledge of scripture, a familiarity which dissenters and reformers of another era
directed to polemical ends. Moralizing governesses, among the
first professionals to write especially for children, also made their
interpretive work unstintingly ideological, through using biblical
characters and texts as paradigms in telling stories aimed at educat-
ing their audience in a sense of virtue. Contemporary efforts to
reemphasize the motherhood of Yahweh and refashion liturgical
language to include all of humanity along with reexaminations of
male-dominated scholarship are the latest extensions in this interpretive chain.

2

Medieval Visionaries:
The Power of Holiness

We are willing to lead thee back and we are unwilling to desert thee, and all the heavenly host rejoices for thee: therefore it becomes us to sing in harmony.

—Hildegard of Bingen,
Ordo Virtutum (The Play of the Virtues)

The soul, too, praises God in six ways:
    You are my mirror-mountain,
    delight of my eyes,
    loss of myself,
    storm of my heart,
    downfall and loss of my strength,
    my highest security.
        —Mechthild of Magdeburg, *Das Fliessende Licht der
            Gottheit (The Flowing Light of Godhead)*

O soul, think that He sustained all of this to save you. . . . It was on a Cross that you heard Jesus Christ began His life, such as the life He led, and it was on a Cross that He finished His life. Why, then, do you delay? Why are you so negligent and so lazy? Why do you hesitate to climb onto the Cross, to stay there and to die on the Cross?

—Angela da Foligno, *bella e utile dottrina
(A Lovely and Useful Instruction)*

Renunciation and Passion

Bernard Tavernier's most recent film, *La Passion de Béatrice* (1988), set in the France of the Hundred Years War, charts the

declining fortunes of the knight François de Cortemare. Two female characters demonstrate vividly the consequences of the in-
creasing violence and utter lack of belief of this defeated warrior:
his capable and unforgivably pious daughter, Béatrice, is horrified
by his incestuous advances, and the white-robed holy woman, initially sustained in her cell by offerings from the village, is burned at
the stake as a witch. Silent yet haunting, this barefoot eremite peers
at the audience with such a penetrating gaze that her fate provides
the film's ultimate statement about the bloodiness and ventral immediacy of the society; as the flames licked at her mud-spattered feet
and her cries of pain were lost in the crowd's shouts of carnival fury,
the horror was so unrelieved that for me the theater seemed to be
filled with the smell of burning. Part of my reaction, I realized, was
due to the fact that Tavernier had allowed us to know something of
this woman and her peaceful, solitary ways; another reason why she
kept preoccupying my thoughts, I concluded later, is that her otherness and humanity kept reminding me of the mystics and visionaries in whose works I was immersed.

Stress on either the singularity or the ordinariness of these
women, on their renunciatory ethic or the passionate, often erotic,
intensity of their writing, can result in a strangely skewed focus.
One of the easiest ways of categorizing and thereby dismissing
these abbesses, nuns, chantresses, beguines, tertiaries, anchorites,
mothers, wives, and widows is to define them in terms of prevailing theological or philosophical fashions. Rarely resorting to Aristotelian or scholastic arguments, unembroiled in the nominalist-
realist controversy, and often unfamiliar with the full range of the
trivium and quadrivium as well as Peter Lombard's *Sentences,* they
existed in the tenuous, anomalous divide between professional theology and lay piety. Never referring to themselves as interpreters
or postillers, they also used no male pseudonyms and felt empow-
ered to write—in first, second, and third person—as preachers,
apostles, mediators, and teachers.

Criticism and Suspicion

Although their concepts of self-mortification might seem ex-
cessive to us, these women were remarkably undeterred by the
negative criticism leveled at them, of which the pronouncement of
Jean Gerson (1363–1420), the poet-chancellor of the University of
Paris, forms a typical example:

All women's teaching, particularly formal teaching by
word and by writing, is to be held suspect unless it has
been diligently examined and much more fully than
men's. The reason is clear: common law—and not any
kind of common law but that which comes from on
high—forbids them. And why? Because they are easily
seduced and determined seducers; and because it is not
proved that they are witnesses to divine grace. (*De examinatione doctrinarum,* pt. 1, 3a)[1]

Not just their teaching but their contemplative lives as well were
subject to close and often suspicious scrutiny. The unknown fourteenth century priest, author of *The Cloud of Unknowing,* offered
withering criticisms of mere spiritual inquisitiveness, which leads
some dilettantes to "strain their whole nervous system in untutored
animal ways" (chapter 45); censoriously he dismissed their staring,
sniggering, squinting, crying, whining, and flailing about as "a sure
sign of pride, perverted knowledge, unregulated showing off and
sinful curiosity" (chapter 53). It took several centuries, though, before good humor marked any commentary on the lives and practices of medieval holy women. Dorothy Sayers is one of the few who
attempts a refreshingly parodic look at their learnedness. Because
some claims about the women's-college atmosphere of the medieval
convent can get very inflated, her 1954 squib for *Punch,* on the
patron saint of pedants, supplies a timely puncturing.

[Saint Supercilia was] a maiden of remarkable erudition,
who steadfastly refused to marry anyone who could not
defeat her in open disputation. When all the best scholars
of all the universities in Europe had tried and failed, her
unworthy father brutally commanded her to accept the
hand of a man who, though virtuous, sensible, and of a
good estate, knew only six languages, and was weak in
mathematics. At this the outraged saint raised her eye-
brows so high that they lifted her right off her feet and
out through a top-storey window, where she was last seen
floating away in a northerly direction. (Brabazon 258)

Aside from the posthumous discovery of manuscripts in some
cases and quibbles over their authenticity in others, the most serious
barrier to scholarly consideration of their work is the belittlement

which, before the last few decades, used to characterize critical comments. William James' judgment, in 1902, that their religious experiences were "theopathic, absurd, and puerile" (275), and William Inge's 1906 assessment of Gertrude of Helfta's work as "a paltry record of sickly compliments and semi-erotic endearments" (52), convey some of the distaste—provoked, no doubt, by a keen sense of embarrassment over the women's flouting of the standards of devotional and theological decorum. Even John Bugge's fairly recent study (1975) of the medieval "ideal of virginity" as a form of "ontological asexuality" (80) still betrays a certain uneasiness, when he considers how the erotic epithalamial motifs, with their allegorical meanings for male virgins, were "adopted in a provocatively literal sense by women" (92). Perceptions and, in some instances, exaltations of consecrated virginity continue to provide differing responses. For Thomas Renna this medieval ideal was "a symbol of renunciation and resolution" (86); for Sharon Elkins, a "guarantee of freedom" (29); and for Sister Margaret Brennan, "the pursuance of a disembodied spirituality" (40).

In Their Own Context

Many of the features of medieval philosophical discourse can actually serve to describe the diverse work of these religious women. With no access to cathedral schools or universities, they were convent-educated for the most part, but far from the unlettered spinners, sewers, and embroiderers whom Urbain le Courtois recommended as the ideal wives:

> Si femme volez esposer
> Pensez de lei, mon fils chier
> Pernez nule por sa beauté
> Ni ki soit en livre lettrié;
> Car sovent sunt decevables.

(If you wish to marry, my son, remember this: choose no women for their beauty or learning, because they are often deceitful.)[2]

On the contrary, these accomplished women were living incarnations of the liberal arts sculpted on so many cathedral façades; they combined in varying ways Grammar's rod of correction, Rhetoric's tablets of poetry, and Dialectic's serpent of wisdom, with arithmetical counting, geometrical and astronomical measurements, and musical bell-ringing.

The convents where most of them lived were more than a refuge for those avoiding arranged marriages and numerous pregnancies. Yet some historians insist that this independence was precisely the convent's attraction. In commenting on the determination of the recluse Christina of Markyate to outwit her family's marriage plans, Sharon Elkins maintains, in *Holy Women of Twelfth-Century England,* that virginity's fundamental importance was its provision of freedom—from affianced matches, risky confinements, and unintellectual domesticity. However, because of a deep faith and an assured sense of vocation, as many, if not more, women wished for and warmly embraced the religious life from a very early age. In addition, like the holy women of the patristic period, whom Elizabeth Clark has surveyed in *Ascetic Piety and Women's Faith,* these women discovered, in their renunication and "more rigorous religious praxis" (ix), the stimulus for "the building of a new Christian society" (x). Hildegard of Bingen, the tenth child of pious parents, was promised—literally tithed—to the church by the time she was eight, and took vows by fifteen. Far from being decrepit or forsaken, convents—especially those in Germany—were centers of advancement and scholarship. The lack of "high social status," as in many of the religious communities studied by Elkins, resulted in "canons and monks exercis(ing) more control over religious women" (162) than would seem to have been the norm in most continental institutions. Often of aristocratic lineage, nuns were usually from wealthy, dowry-paying families. The abbess at Gandersheim held her own court of law, coined her own money, and had a seat in the imperial diet. Hildegard's convent on the slope of the Rupertsberg on the Rhine near Bingen had running water and a handsomely appointed scriptorium. The convent at Helfta, where Gertrude the Great, Mechthild of Hackeborn, and Mechthild of Magdeburg all lived and wrote, was known throughout Germany in the thirteenth century "as a house of piety and learning" (Halligan 33).

The learning promoted in this and most other religious communities of women, indebted though it was to male counselors and advisors and obedient to the hierarchy and magisterium, was nevertheless significantly different from the prevailing Thomistic urge to reduce to unity (*reducere ad unum*). Diverse in subject and approach, medieval women's writing also often worked through an underlying dialectic, which addressed the reader or engaged an interlocutor. Rather than contribute to the scholastic exercise of teasing arcane meanings out of such terms as *esse, unum, bonum,* and *verum,* their work was an unorthodox combination of immediacy, purposiveness, and intensely personal, speculative probing into the mysteries involved in Godhead, redemption, and eschatology. Acknowledging the lures of ignorance, sin, and mortality, their work demonstrated the antidotes of wisdom, virtue, and action—in the terms of Vincent de Beauvais' *Imago Mundi: philosophia theorica, philosophia practica,* and *philosophia mechanica* (theoretical, practical, and mechanical subjects or systems). That many of these writers were likely unaware of Vincent de Beauvais' work in no way diminishes this claim, nor does it lessen the particularity of their examination of truth, the right way of living, and the needs of the body. In a similar vein, although very few had read Aristotle's *De Interpretatione,* they would have been just as unlikely to contest its main premise about the signifying qualities of speech and writing. They would have agreed with Aristotle that "spoken sounds are symbols of affections in the soul, and written marks symbols of spoken sounds" (I, 25).

Varying Forms of Interpretation

The variety of their responses to the Vulgate, which in most cases they were able to read, best reveals the distinctive self-confidence and lyricism of medieval women's "interpretive" work. Based on their knowledge of the real world of castle, convent, Beguine group, or household, they saw in the Bible enticements to liturgical celebration, models and warnings of behavior, invitations to word games and numerological explanations, supports for faith, and foundations for visionary experience. After an exhaustive catalogue of friar exegetes, in *The Study of the Bible in the Middle Ages,* Beryl Smalley observes that "at some time in the thirteenth century commentators step back 'through the looking-glass,' out of their world of reflection into everyday life" (308). Women interpreters, though excluded from most surveys of exegesis, never forgot the everyday life. Scripture was a way of illuminating the here and now. Like the brilliantly multi-colored and treasured illuminated Bibles of their time, scripture for them, "written to be read aloud, amplifies its meaning by metamorphosing into icon—concrete, cyclical, historical, vibrating with carefully harmonized chords of meaning" (Happ 441).

It would be a distortion, however, to suggest greater uniformity among them. Spanning periods of patristic, scholastic, and secular authorities, their writings and dictations reflect the community life of cenobitic Benedictinism, the rise of mendicant piety and its attack on clerical corruption, and the differing vogues of unenclosed urban communities devoted to charitable works and contemplative withdrawal. The continuum moves from the scholarly plays of the canoness Hrotsvitha of Gandersheim and the abbess Hildegard of Bingen, to the affective spirituality of the visions and prayers of Gertrude of Helfta, Mechthild of Hackeborn, and Mechthild of Magdeburg; from the renunciation and self-criticism of the Franciscan Blessed Angela da Foligno, the Dominican St. Catherine of Siena, and the Beguine Hadewijch, to the meditations in the midst of a bustling world of the autobiographer Margery Kempe and the anchorite Julian of Norwich.

Warnings about the unwieldiness of surveying such a large span of time come from many quarters. Barbara Newman prefaces her brilliant study of the sapiential theology of Hildegard of Bingen with the sobering observation that "it can be misleading to study female saints as if they formed a subculture unto themselves, isolated from the overwhelmingly male culture that surrounded them" (xv). Although she predicts little benefit from seeing a particular figure "as part of a 'female tradition,' " I think the undertaking can be defended on several counts. Rather than theorizing about a non-existent subculture of religious women, studying the tradition of women's work forces the reader to assess this highly idiosyncratic writing in light of the conditions—of the religious order and of the lay world—on which it frequently commented. Charting such a continuum also makes it clear that, for these women, interpreting or commenting on the Bible changed from a natural, un-self-conscious activity to a self-conscious and ultimately polemical one. Their use of the traditional humility topos, picturing themselves as fragile vessels and sinful creatures notwithstanding, they did reach peaks of assurance and self-awareness at various points. And, again, conditions in their culture usually accounted for these developments.

Although their text was, in general, the Vulgate, they often related the lessons or precepts which they gleaned from it orally. These influences are also discernible in their writing, normally in a vernacular suffused and imbricated with biblical pericopes and allusions as a common ground. Another feature, which I discovered through the great good fortune of working with graduate students in declaiming and dramatizing some of these texts, was the sonorous quality of the words and their built-in performance value. We felt that these medieval women, acutely aware though they were of the power of the pulpit, also perceived the compelling, emotive magnetism of the theater—in using symbolism to depict the battlefield of the soul, or relying on a curtained enclosure to present everyday exchanges and political schemes. Furthermore, by letting the women speak in their own voices, we became more aware of these mystics and visionaries as distinct individuals in comparison with a host of popular literary fabrications and recreations. Less corrupted by the "wormwood of office" (244) than the nuns of Syliva Townsend Warner's fictional medieval religious house, in *The Corner That Held Them* (1948), these religious never seemed to be mired in pettiness.

Growth of Scholarship in the Area

Sources proudly affirmative of women's work are growing in number, and the revisionist tenor of recent scholarship in the field is encouraging, too. Over the past five years the appearance of a half dozen anthologies of writing by medieval women, medieval visionaries, renaissance women, and seventeenth century women poets shows that the work of exhuming these texts has acquired a real momentum. In addition, a critical eye is being focused on many of the embedded and inherently misogynist views about, or applied to, medieval religious women. Isidore of Seville's *Etymologiae*, concerning the state of man, affords a classic instance:

> *Vir noncupatus, quod major in eo vis est, quam in femina. Unde et virtus nomen accepit, sive quod vi agat feminam. Mulier vero, a mollitie, tanquam mollier, detracta littera, vel mutata, appellata est mulier. Sed ideo virtus maxima viri, mulieris minor.* (Lib. XI. caput ii. 17–19; *PL* 82, 418)

> He is called "man" (*vir*) because there is greater "strength" in him than in women: whence "virtue" takes its name. . . . But "woman" (*mulier*) comes from "softness" (*mollitie*) . . . therefore there is greater virtue in man and less in woman.[3]

Several modern studies start from exactly the opposite premise. Far from being scandalized by the "emotionalism" of the mystic experience, Ioan Lewis' *Ecstatic Religion* considers the various social functions of spirit possession and Shamanism, clarifying from the outset that "peripheral possession" is neither "a secure female monopoly" nor the result of "any innate tendency to hysteria on the part of women" (32). Victor Turner's examination of metaphors in religious culture, in *Dramas, Fields, and Metaphors*, stresses the positive connotations of "anti-structure" or "*communitas*" as "a generative center . . . representing the desire for a total, unmediated relationship between person and person" (273, 274); such terminology might explain some of the spontaneous, immediate, concrete nature of the visionary's experience within the institutionalized, constraining structure of medieval religion. In *Woman as Image in Medieval Literature* Joan Ferrante looks at another form of doubleness, arguing that "when men think of desirable qualities as female, even as female impulses in themselves . . . they exalt female figures in literature . . . [but] when they think of women as real beings, they tend to see them only as child-bearers, or as temptresses" (13).

Other studies concentrate on specific texts, explicating how these women understood themselves and constructed imaginative worlds. Peter Dronke's *Women Writers of the Middle Ages* concludes that their work was deliberately personalized, characterized by "a lack of apriorism, of predetermined postures," and by "attempts to cope with human problems in their singularity—not imposing rules and categories from without, but seeking solutions that are apt and truthful existentially" (x). He presents a convincing argument for the "supersubtle" and "distinctive literary coquetry" (83) of the Canoness Hrotsvitha, who used Terentian themes for Christian purposes in her dramas, and mines the letters of the Rhenish Sibyl, the Abbess Hildegard, to demonstrate how "daunting and eccentric" she was: "stupendous in her powers of thought and expression; lovable in her warmth and never-wearying freshness in everything she tackled" (201). These texts remain for Dronke sources of wonder and inspiration.

Caroline Walker Bynum's studies of women's devotional literature and practice disclose many of the tensions underlying medieval religious life. *Jesus as Mother* focuses on the problem of authority as reflected in various attempts at the feminization of religious language, and the more recent *Holy Feast and Holy Fast* sees the particular piety of medieval holy women oscillating between eucharistic worship and total abstinence from nourishment. The speciality and separateness of these women are Bynum's concerns. While the abbot could envision his role as a maternal one and often pray to a feminine God, lay women and actual mothers were usually dismissed as carnal and secondary. It is not surprising that female spirituality stayed on the periphery of male-dominated scholastic theology. Yet female eucharistic devotions and ascetic lifestyles also form an instructive contrast to the satires of monastic greed and gluttony, and account for the striking fact that "many important treatises on the eucharist or on the closely connected theme of the humanity of Christ were addressed by men to women" (*Feast,* 80). Although Bynum contends that "the delicious groveling in the humiliations of being human . . . characterizes virtually every religious woman of the later Middle Ages" (290), she stresses the deliberate purposiveness of their elaboration of aspects from biological or social experience, because these vehicles best reflected "the deepening of ordinary experience that came when God impinged on it" (295).

In two studies of medieval sainthood the emphasis is not on calm or integrated self-awareness, but on turbulent dualism and cringing self-negation. Donald Weinstein and Rudolph Bell cast a wide net, surveying saints from the eleventh to the seventeenth centuries, with the central understanding that "saints stood as a reproach to the wonder-seeking crowd even as they served its humble needs" (5). The analysis of data-filled tables, in *Saints and Society,* is as revealing as the explained differences between male and female saints. In contrast to the predominantly male saints of the eleventh to twelfth centuries, modeled on the figures of the bishop and the reformer so crucial to the period of the Cluniac reform, the investiture controversy, and the crusades, the thirteenth century witnessed a doubling in the percentage of women saints, attributable both to the faltering of traditional male leadership and to the broadening of the social base for sainthood, as encouraged by the rise of the mendicant orders and new forms of piety. While the proportion of women saints remained high in the fourteenth and fifteenth centuries, it dropped sharply in the sixteenth century with the reaffirmation of traditional authority and hierarchy during the reformation period.

Weinstein and Bell's study is largely statistical; individual cases or histories are less important in themselves and more significant as examples of a specific group or category. The authors also rely on contrast (with the greater sampling of males) and compensation (for ecclesiastical and social barriers) to explain such manifestations of female religiousness as a seven year old's visions, an adolescent's longing for Christ as a bridegroom, and a married woman's torment by demons. As Weinstein and Bell look at the women's reactions "to society's more subtle yet pervasive definition of womanhood" (229), they underline the psychic and compensatory rationales of these phenomena:

> The girl's vision was a weapon she used in her struggle against the destiny her parents were shaping for her; the young maiden's choice of Christ as her bridegroom relieved her of the burden of taking a worldly husband; the matron's demonic assaults were the products of guilt and depression arising from a life imposed upon her and from which she longed to escape. (229)

Rather than emphasizing the contrasts between social expectations and individual goals, Richard Kieckhefer, in his examination of fourteenth century saints, *Unquiet Souls*, highlights other dichotomies: between life on earth and a yearned-for life in heaven, between rapturous, ecstatic illumination and excruciating guilt for having occasioned the passion and death of Christ, and between patient forbearance and self-inflicted pain. Finding it impossible to "refrain from judgment in the face of what appears to be obsessive guilt, effusive emotional devotion, and masochistic asceticism" (197), Kieckhefer develops his theorizing about these tortured souls, "painfully ill at ease with the world and with themselves" (201), around the central motif of disquietude.

The tense, embattled aspect of many of these women's lives cannot be denied. Yet their transcendent, salvific belief in the mysteries of the redemption and the resurrection must not be forgotten either. A remarkably common feature of their writing is the ways in which they use biblical precepts and allusions to define, support, and proselytize about this hard-won hope.

Hrotsvitha of Gandersheim

If this tenth century canoness, who had taken vows of chastity and obedience, set out to interpret any text, it was to rewrite the comedies of Terence with a distinctly Christian emphasis. Although she made use of such sources as a fourth century legend ascribed to the Syrian Ephrem, Rufinus' *Historia Monachorum*, and the apocryphal *Acts of John*, and borrowed theories from Augustine, Boethius, and Cassiodorus among others, the text providing the discipline, on which all of her six plays in rhymed, rhythmic

Latin prose were based, was the Bible. Direct quotations from the Vulgate are rare in Hrotsvitha's plays, but their reliance on scriptural symbology, paralleling of biblical episodes, and emulation of the psalmist's plea lend an undeniable authority to her depictions of conversion, repentance, and martyrdom. By embodying so many scriptural lessons her dramas personalize the central tenets of sacrifice and salvation.

Hrotsvitha entered the community at Gandersheim as a well-read young woman in her early twenties. In her writing, which consists of versified legends of the saints, a panegyric of Otto I, a history of Gandersheim, and thirty-five hexameters describing scenes from Revelation as well as the dramas, she pays tribute to the tutelage of the nun Rikkardis, the abbess Gerberga (niece of Otto I), and learned clergymen. Despite her knowledge of cosmopolitan culture and probable acquaintance with life at the imperial court, the repeated theme in Hrotsvitha's anti-Terentian plays is not the amorous schemes of worldly young men but the laudable chastity of Christian virgins. The Preface makes clear her intention to use Scripture to supplant pagan sophistries and promote virtue over lasciviousness.

> Many Catholics one may find,/ and we are also guilty of charges of this kind,/ who for the beauty of their eloquent style,/ prefer the uselessness of pagan guile/ to the usefulness of sacred Scripture./ There are also others, who, devoted to Sacred reading and scorning the works of other pagans, yet frequently read Terence's fiction,/ and as they delight in the sweetness of his style and diction,/ they are stained by learning of wicked things in his depiction./ Therefore I, the Forceful Testimony of Gandersheim, have not refused to imitate him in writing/ whom others laud in reading,/ so that in that self-same form of composition in which the shameless acts of lascivious women were phrased/ the laudable chastity of sacred virgins be praised/ within the limits of my little talent.[4]

The praise of women and the seeming self-abasement are intricately interrelated. Deliberately contrasting the six Terentian comedies, in which women succumb to the ploys of amorous pagans, the action of Hrotsvitha's plays will center on mainly pure and upright women. In her opening letter to patrons, Hrotsvitha is entirely aware of her use of the Pauline motif of being what she is by the grace of God—her *deum . . . cuius solummodo gratia sum id, quod sum* echoing Paul's *gratia autem Dei sum id quod sum* (1 Cor 15:10)—as well as the recurring idea of confounding strength with weakness (1 Cor 1:27; 4:10; 15:43; 2 Cor 12:9). She makes the paradox of mere women triumphing as acceptable as the claim made by one of limited female intellect (*"muliebris sensus tardior"*) to appropriate a Boethian stance and tear small pieces from Philosophy's robe (*"floccos de panniculis, a veste philosophiae abruptis"*). In teaching the reader to savor the rich ambiguities of the erudition and wit of this supposedly limited writer, for whom "each admission of weakness is inseparable from an impulse of self-assurance" (Dronke, *Women Writers,* 66), Hrotsvitha thereby prepares the reader for a comparable reversal of expectations in the plays themselves.

While the critical literature generally acknowledges her erudition and determination as a pedagogue, opinions are actually quite divided about the nature of Hrotsvitha's accomplishment. No one now endorses the position of the nineteenth century Viennese von Aschbach who claimed that Hrotsvitha's plays were a hoax, perpetrated by their real writer, Conrad Celtis, the renaissance editor and discoverer of the Emmeram codex of Hrotsvitha's works. Hailing her as "a Christian Sappho" (1), Albert Cohn has charted similarities with Shakespeare, and Rosamond Gilder has introduced her as "the first woman playwright" (18). Countering such praise are George Coffman's dismissal of the notion that her dialogues were ever acted as a "fallacy" (262), Karl Young's estimate that her plays were "never acted and probably little read" (6), and Philip Allen's grand slam that "she not only could not write a drama, she did not think of doing so" (43). Daniel Frankforter has pinpointed the sexist problem inherent in many of the niggling comments: "The fact that she was a woman who wrote dramas at a time when dramas were not supposed to have been written and women not equipped with educations adequate to achieve what she achieved made it difficult to place her work in a context which would facilitate its interpretation" (299).

Amazingly one of the issues which still exercises the ever-increasing Hrotsvitha scholars (two separate English translations[5] of her plays have appeared in the last decade) is the performance or mere closet study value of her work. That is, did the canoness who set out to praise the power of female chastity intend her plays as pious refectory reading or complete, humane, albeit fast-moving entertainments about the ministry of love in action? I submit that this "strong voice of Gandersheim," as a self-conscious elocutionist and scholar, also felt deeply about the role of emotions and human attachments in the inculcation of religious precepts; as Jakob Grimm recognized, she even punned on her own name by calling herself *ego clamor validus Gandeshemensis,* a Latinization of her old Saxon name (hruot= *clamor;* sui(n)d= *validus*). Because her plays cry out for performance, the delight of Anatole France at seeing a marionette version, Ellen Terry's participation in a 1920s London West End production of *Paphnutius,* the spirited defenses of her first translator into English prose, "Christopher St. John" (Cristabel Marshall), of Rosamond Gilder, and Edwin Zeydel, and the revisionist scholarship of her most modern commentator and translator, Katharina Wilson, are all plausible and understandable. Even without costumes and props, the didactic energy of Hrotsvitha's plays impresses both Charles Jones and Peter Dronke as made for recitation, whether in the classroom-style assignment of "speaking parts" imagined by Jones (102) or the community "reading groups" suggested by Dronke (*Poetic Individuality,* 85). Wilson's book-length study, which locates Hrotsvitha within the scholastic traditions of the tenth century Ottonian renaissance, favors the performance thesis by citing the frequent visits to Gandersheim of Otto II's cultured wife, the Byzantine princess Theophano. Furthermore, Wilson concludes that Hrotsvitha's ethical stance is the affirmation of an "absolutist epistemology," where truth is "recognizable . . . eternal, and imitable"; but she insists that the formulation of this ethic is more dynamic than intellectual: "provoking an emotional response, persuading one to act" (143).

The immeasurable power of women's virtue and, in fact, women's capacity to reform their own lives are the repeated ideas in all six plays. Frankforter makes many claims about the prominence and potential of women in Hrotsvitha's work. Writing on the canoness' contribution to "the destiny of women," he remarks that of the approximately twenty women on whom her work focuses, only one (the adulterous wife of St. Gongolf) is an unrepentant sinner. When he sketches the "thematic structure" of her plays as options for Christian heroism, Frankforter concentrates on the published order, based on the St. Emmeram manuscript, as Hrotsvitha's analysis of "the feminine condition in six logically successive and increasingly complex stages":

> 1) the young girl who chooses virginity over marriage ["Gallicanus"]; 2) the virgin whose desire to remain unmarried is not accepted by those in power over her ["Agapes,

Chionia and Hirena"]; 3) the woman who marries but emulates the life of a nun in her marriage ["Calimachus"]; 4) the nun who falls into sin and loses her faith, her religious profession and her virginity ["Mary"]; 5) the whore who willingly adopts a life of vice and wantonness ["Thais"]; and 6) the woman who surrenders her virginity for the vocation of Christian motherhood ["Fides, Spes and Karitas"]. (226)

Although the following examination of the motifs of conversion, repentance, and martyrdom does not follow the manuscript order, it also underscores the virtues and capacities of women, which Hrotsvitha has emphasized adroitly through biblical allusions and models.

The plays forever confound worldly or, more correctly, pagan attitudes. In "The Conversion of the General Gallicanus" the virginal force of Constantia, daughter of the emperor, is great enough to convert her betrothed, Gallicanus, to Christianity as well as celibacy. Furthermore, despite the efforts of the persecutor Julian to reverse the liberality of Constantine's reign by perverting the point of a biblical injunction (Lk 14:33), the play closes with the double baptism of Julian's henchman and this functionary's son. Curiously, this single biblical quotation, cited tauntingly by Julian, highlights, in a way the pagan could not understand, the renunciation of sin involved in the baptisms of Gallicanus, Terentianus, and his son. Julian deliberately uses the words of Christ (*sententiam Christi*) to justify seizure of the Christians' property, as he commands his soldiers:

> *obiciendo sententiam Christi, dicentis: 'Qui non renuntiaverit omnibus, quae possidet, non potest meus esse discipulus.'*

> Quote Christ's words to those who object: "Whosoever he be of you that forsaketh not all he hath, he cannot be my disciple."

His choice of the Lucan passage reduces Julian to the level of the fault-finding Pharisees who miss the point about the kingdom of God, which reverses legalistic expectations to allow for curing on the sabbath and feasting with the poor.

Hrotsvitha's second conversion play, "The Resurrection of Drusiana and Calimachus," shows how faith can cool both lust and necrophilia. Biblical allusions and particularly psalmic utterances for deliverance and peace are prominent throughout. In announcing the resurrection motif the Prologue borrows the important term "reborn" (*renatus*) from John 3:3 to describe the lusting Calimachus as eventually "*resuscitatus, in Christo . . . renatus*" (resurrected and reborn in Christ). Calimachus' desperate affection so unnerves the chaste matron Drusiana that, like the Psalmist, she pleads for help and direction:

> *Intende, domine, mei timorem;/ intende, quem patior, dolorem! /*
> *Quid mihi, quid agendum sit, ignoro.*

> Oh, Lord, look upon my fear,/ look upon the pain I bear!/
> I don't know what to do.

The action is rapid-fire: Drusiana dies immediately; Calimachus attempts to violate her corpse and is killed by a snake; but, thanks to the intercession of the apostle Saint John, he and Drusiana are brought back to life. What saves the play from the ludicrousness which this summary implies are the poignancy of Calimachus' repentance and the zeal of John's sermonizing. In a positive sense they slow down and comment upon the action, and they rely heavily on biblical allusions and dicta. Recalling the Miserere (Ps 50/51) and the supplications of the "overcome" and "distraught" sinner whose "heart is in anguish" (Ps 54/55), Calimachus implores:

> Oh, if I could only open the secret door/ of my inmost
> heart and soul/ so that you could see the bitter anguish of
> my suffering, and take pity on the patient.

By contrast the apostle, awestruck before the Lord's majesty and compassion, reflects the psalms of praise and a New Testament faith in his prayer.

> O Christ, the world's redeemer, Thou Who suffered for
> us sinners, I know not how to praise Thee/ how to glorify
> Thee:/ I am overcome by thy kind mercy and Thy merciful patience.

The stress on divine mercy is constant in John's speeches; he actually follows the request of the Pater Noster about forgiveness—*et dimitte nobis debita nostra, sicut et nos dimittimus debitoribus nostris:* and

forgive us our debts as we also have forgiven our debtors (Mt
6:12)—in formulating this "law of our religion":

> *ut homo homini dimittat,/ si ipse a deo dimitti ambiat:* to forgive
> those who trespass against us if we hope that God forgives
> us our trespasses against him.

The unforgiving and unforgiven transgressor is the *"infelicissimus"*
(most unfortunate) Fortunatus, who had opened Drusiana's grave.
John's explanation of Fortunatus' banishment "from the flock of
God-fearing men" refers to the parable of the evil shoot producing
bitter fruit; his comparison, *"malae arbori/ amaros fructus facienti,"*
imitates Matthew's account of the warning about knowing false
prophets by their fruit: *mala autem arbor malos fructus facit* (the bad
tree bears evil fruit [7.17]).

But the most compelling plays, those which genuinely cry out
for performance in my estimate, concern prostitutes reclaimed by
monks from brothels. "The Fall and Repentance of Mary" and "The
Conversion of the Harlot Thais" are also the dramas where
Hrotsvitha's use of biblical allusion and symbol is most pervasive
and subtle. In "Mary" the heroine's uncle, Abraham, manages the
conversion motif. The visions which torment this saintly monk after
his niece's disappearance from her cell do not require the discernment of a Joseph or a Daniel to be interpreted; he sees "a dragon of
miraculous size and of foul smell" seizing "a little white dove" and a
wolf snatching a lamb. In rescuing his charge from these predators,
Abraham, like the redeemer, takes her sins upon himself, and, like
the good shepherd, leads "her back, rejoicing, to the fold." Because
repentance involves circular action, his intercession, through a temporary transfer of roles, returns her to the position of *stella maris,*
the star of the sea, which is the bright light that guides sailors in the
right path ("*navigantibus recti semitam itineris dirigit*" [II,3]). The
lengthy "*stella-maris*" etymology lesson at the outset of the play, in
which Abraham and his fellow monk Effrem had encouraged the
eight year old Mary to embrace the eremetical, ascetic life, though
not found in Hrotsvitha's source (a sixth century Latin version of an
earlier Syrian legend), "stands fully in the liturgical and hymnal
tradition of the medieval church"; "as the *stella maris* leads ships
safely to the home port, to their destination, so Maria, too, shall be
guided home" (Wilson, "Lesson," 3). As well as setting in motion the
interest in Marian virtues, such an emphasis also forecasts Hrotsvitha's preoccupation with repentance rather than the few lines

devoted to the fall, which is the *fait accompli* of Mary's jumping out of her window to join a deceiving lover.

Virtue is again triumphant in reclaiming Thais, and here, too, Hrotsvitha's adaptation of her source material prefigures the drama's themes of reconciliation and concord. In the opening lesson between the hermit Paphnutius and his disciples, she draws liberally on Boethius' *De Musica.* As David Chamberlain has argued, the play's interweaving of this quadrivial learning with its moral action "shows Pafnutius . . . bringing the discordant sinner Thais back to the norms of concord or *musica humana*" (321). Moreover, Hrotsvitha's biblical allusions and citations corroborate the need for spiritual harmony. Although the dumbfounded disciples comment on Paphnutius' musical theorizing by quoting almost verbatim Paul's observation in 1 Corinthians 1:27, *nam stulta mundi elegit deus, ut confunderet sophistica:* God has chosen the foolish to confound the wise, the hermit encourages them to be bold in pursuing knowledge of the divine arrangement, "*in numero et mensura et pondere*" (according to number, measure, and weight), echoing Wisdom 11:21 directly as he does so. Thais is actually a more fit subject for his pedagogy than the disciples; since she already knows that God "weighs the merits of each person justly in His scale," her "conversion" is more of an opportunity for discussion of her beliefs than any radical alteration of them. A stern and unrelenting mentor, Paphnutius introduces his now-penitent charge to the abbess as "a half-dead little she-goat" who "having cast aside the rough pelt of a goat . . . will be clothed with the soft wool of the lamb." While this allusion may remind the listener that the Torah's sacrifice for a sin of ignorance was a she-goat (Num 15:27), the evangelist's account of the sheep divided from and privileged over the goats (Mt 25:32–34) could also be recalled. The final biblical emphasis promotes and sustains a trust in forgiveness, for Paphnutius' next encounter, after an interval of three years, with the thoroughly remorseful, immured Thais provides the self-doubting woman with necessary hope. His observation, "*Si deus iniquitates observabit, / nemo sustinebit,*" is an apt borrowing from the *De Profundis:* "If thou, O Lord, shouldst mark iniquities, Lord, who could stand?" (Ps 129/130:3); it also tempers his righteousness, allowing more pastoral concern to shine through.

As doughty challengers of Terentian *mores,* Hrotsvitha's plays continue to celebrate the virtues of women—both those saved from harlotry and those steadfastly devoted to goodness who are martyred for being staunch. In "The Martyrdom of Agapes,

Chionia, and Hirena," the virginal trio, representing Charity, Purity, and Peace, stands as obstinate counters to Diocletian, Dulcitius, and Sissinus and their associations with passion, sin and death. Sandro Sticca has maintained that the drama, in which at one point the besotted Dulcitius attempts to make love to pots and pans, is much more than farce; but such a scene does exemplify Hrotsvitha's shrewd dramaturgical sense in reducing sin to slapstick comedy. Yet the slaughter of the virgins, comparable to that of Fides, Spes, and Karitas at the behest of the maddened Emperor Hadrian in the last play ("The Martyrdom of the Holy Virgins Fides, Spes, and Karitas"), magnifies the differences between virtuous and worldly ways, the overarching theme of all the dramas.

The straightness and narrowness of this path to virtue, which brooks little or no traffic with the world, probably account for some of the dismissive comments of readers critical of Hrotsvitha's moral precision or dramatic purposiveness, or both. Few would go as far as John Kennedy Toole's hero in *The Confederacy of Dunces*, the obese medievalist Ignatius Reilly, who dreams,

> Were Hrosvitha with us today, we would all look to her for counsel and guidance. From the austerity and tranquility of her medieval world, the penetrating gaze of this legendary Sybil of a holy nun would exorcise the horrors which materialize before our eyes in the name of television. (64)

The madcap fury with which Reilly dashes off his discontent with modernity in Big Chief writing tablets bears no resemblance to Hrotsvitha's measured, faith-suffused, and biblically inspired assault on Terence. The closing lines of her descriptions based on Revelation supply, I think, a more illuminating summary of the devices, intentions, and promises of her dramas; as Edwin Zeydel translates:

> Here behold the lamb standing on the Mount Zion
> And the host of virgins chanting new hymns.
> This beast attacks the saints with the power of a dragon.
> Truth coming forth on a white horse laid it low;
> He lashes the old dragon to fierce Tartarus.
> Lo, the books of life are held open to the dead,
> And quickened they arise who had been shackled by death.
> Presently all are given their rewards according to their
>   works.

Hildegard of Bingen

Less concerned with meting out rewards and punishments or with modeling moral conduct, the voice of Hildegard of Bingen (1098–1179) is at once prophetic and hymnal. The universe she sees is symphonic, its enclosure of light and dark testifying to the honest wholeness of her vision; its energies, vital and kinetic, are also manifestations of the immanence of the divine presence. Because her writing is fundamentally exegetical and visionary, the Bible for Hildegard does more than tessellate her work; specific texts are often the departure points for lengthy, at times convoluted, divagations on the sense of universal life in a world aflame with mysterious yet omnipresent divinity. Furthermore, like the Old Testament prophets, she makes her densely symbolic language a vehicle for conveying warnings or instructions to lay and clerical leaders of her day. Despite her frequent protestations about female weakness, her hymns and prose bristle with a fervor that is distinctly purposive and self-assured. Though suffering extended and debilitating illnesses, she wrote three visionary treatises, *Scivias* (Know the Ways), *Liber vitae meritorum* (The Book of Life's Rewards), and *Liber divinorum operum* also called *De operatione Dei* (The Book of Divine Works), as well as a collection of sixty-nine songs, *Symphonia harmoniae caelestium revelationum* (The Symphony of the Harmony of Heavenly Revelations), the first liturgical morality play, *Ordo Virtutum* (The Play of the Virtues), which follows the hymns sequence in one of the two manuscripts of her work, treatises on natural science and medicine known as the *Physica* and *Causae et Curae,* and, showing the encyclopedic range of her curiosity, a secret language and alphabet in *Lingua ignota* and *Litterae ignotae.*

Hildegard was an active and a capable administrator. She studied under the abbess Jutta von Spanheim at the Benedictine monastery of Disibodenberg where, after the abbess' death, she herself was elected as the head. Hildegard corresponded with Frederick Barbarossa and Bernard of Clairvaux, initiated the move of her sisters to the convent at Bingen which she had planned, and embarked on several preaching tours along the Nahe, Main, Moselle, and Rhine rivers. Moreover, she was recognized and appealed to as an authority and a seer; the revelations, which she had experienced from childhood, were sanctified as a prophetic charism by Pope Eugenius III. Theologians, musicians, and historians continue to marvel at the range and unpredictability of her genius.

"Even David made his prophecies good with music," Hildegard observes toward the end of the *Scivias* (Hozeski 391). In fact, her antiphons, sequences, and hymns with neumatic notations, designed for the trained choristers at Bingen who sang canonical hours and liturgies, show some of the ways in which biblical models and symbols inform Hildegard's vision. Her concern throughout is the ubiquity and goodness of God—whether manifest in the paternal direction of salvation history or in the feminine designations of Caritas, Sapientia, and Ecclesia. Such an awareness of divinity accounts for her reliance on music to energize and inspire an audience:

> Just as the power of God flies everywhere and surrounds all things—with nothing resisting it—so also the rationality of people holds great strength for listening to the sounds of living voices. And the soul of people can be aroused from sluggishness to watchfulness by a muscial performance. (Part III, Vision Thirteen: 13)

She was a lifelong supporter of these performances; in her eighty-first year, when her convent was under a temporary interdict during which music was forbidden, she directed these genuinely pastoral comments to the prelates of Mainz, reminding them of music's reflection of an eschatological, redemptive hope:

> I heard a voice from the living light tell of the diverse kinds of praises, of which David says in the Psalms: "Praise him in the call of the trumpet, praise him on psaltery and lute, praise him on the tambour and in dancing, praise him on strings and on organ, praise him on resonant cymbals, praise him on cymbals of jubilation—let every spirit praise the Lord!"
>
> In these words outer realities teach us about inner ones—namely how, in accordance with the material composition and quality of instruments, we can best transform and shape the performance of our inner being towards praises of the Creator. . . . (Dronke, *Women Writers*, 197)

Hildegard seizes on the blending of texts and instruments in songs of praise, specifically enjoined in Psalm 150, as the metaphorical explanation of the uninterrupted line of witnesses to the

word, stretching from the prophets, apostles, martyrs, and priests
to holy women.

> Praise God with the lyre of profound devotion and with
> the harp of a soft-flowing sound. Just as the trumpet is
> played before the lyre, and the lyre is played before the
> harp, likewise also the prophets first rose up in the won-
> drous voices of the blessed angels who persevered in the
> love of truth. And then the prophets spoke through cre-
> ated people, to be followed by the apostles who spoke
> with the sweetest words.
> And praise God with the timbrel of mortification and
> with the dance of exultation. For after the harp, the tim-
> brel exults; after the timbrel the dance follows. Similarly,
> after the apostles prophesied the words of salvation, the
> martyrs suffered various bodily punishments in honor of
> God. And from the martyrs, the truthful teachers of the
> priestly office rose up.
> Praise God with the strings of human redemption and
> with the organ of divine protection. When strings are
> played, the voices of both the strings and the organ are
> heard. Similarly, the virgins went out as true teachers when
> they showed the truth in the office of their blessedness.
> And the virgins loved the Word of God as a true human—
> the strings—and they adored the Word as true God—the
> organ. (*Scivias,* Part Three, Vision Thirteen: 16)

A conspicuous subject in the hymns themselves, whose "inherent parallelism" (563) Barbara Grant has compared to the Hebrew
psalms, is the power of holiness in woman. A second translator,
Kent Kraft, has observed that the songs' "clustering images," their
overlapping "worlds of concept, sense and symbol," sustain their
"endless shimmer of meaning" (158–159). Although the most recent translator, Barbara Newman, characterizes Hildegard's diction as "sometimes caught uneasily between visionary élan and the
more prosaic discourse of exegesis" (42), Newman is particularly
sensitive to the position accorded Mary in the *Symphonia,* "midway
between God the Father and the Holy Spirit," in what she labels "so
many verbal and musical icons of the Madonna and Child" (59). As
an example of this art I offer both the mellifluous, sonorous Latin
text of a hymn to Mary *"Ave generosa"* (which Margaret Philpot
sings on the record or CD *A feather on the breath of God*), and two

different translations; the first, by Kent Kraft, is an accurate rendering, while the second, by Barbara Newman, captures the exultant ardor of this tribute to the Bride of God in free verse.

Ave generosa,
gloriosa et intacta puella,
Tu pupilla castitatis,
tu materia sanctitatis,
que Deo placuit.

Nam hec superna infusio
in te fuit,
quod supernum Verbum
in te carnem induit.

Tu candidum lilium
quod Deus ante omnem creaturam
inspexit.
O pulcherrima et dulcissima,
quam valde Deus in te delectabatur,
cum amplexionem caloris sui
in te posuit,
ita quod Filius eius
de te lactatus est.

Venter enim tuus gaudium habuit
cum omnis celestis symphonia de te sonuit,
quia virgo Filium Dei portasti,
ubi castitas tua in Deo claruit.

Viscera tua gaudium habuerunt
sicut gramen super quod ros cadit
cum ei viriditatem infundit,
ut et in te factum est,
o mater omnis gaudii.

Nunc omnis ecclesia in gaudio rutilet
ac in symphonia sonet
propter dulcissimam Virginem
et laudabilem Virginem
et laudabilem Mariam,
Dei Genitricem. Amen. (Newman 122)

Hail, glorious Virgin, noble, untouched,
eye of purity,
source of holiness,
delight of God.

For the power poured
into you from on high,
the eternal Word
took flesh in you.

White, gleaming lily,
God looked upon you
before any of his creation.

Most lovely, most sweet,
oh how powerfully God delighted in you,
as he took you hotly in his embrace,
that his son might have suck from thee.

For your belly rejoiced
when all the symphony of heaven
resounded from you,
since you, Virgin, bore the Son of God,
your purity brilliant in God.

And your loins rejoiced
like the grass upon which the dew falls;
when it pours greenness upon it;
so it befell you,
O Mother of all joy.

Now the whole Church shines in joy
and sounds in symphony
for the Virgin most sweet
and Mary the praised, the Mother of God. Amen.
(Kraft 259–260)

In the pupil of chastity's eye
I beheld you
untouched.
Generous maid! Know that it's God
who broods over you.

For heaven flooded you like
unbodied speech
and you gave it a tongue.

Glistening
lily: before all worlds
you lured the supernal one.

How he reveled
in your charms! how your beauty
warmed to his caresses
till you gave your breast to his child.

And your womb held joy when heaven's
harmonies rang from you,
a maiden with child by God,
for in God your chastity blazed.

Yes your flesh held joy like the grass
when the dew falls, when heaven
freshens its green: O mother
of gladness, verdure of spring.

Ecclesia, flush with rapture! Sing
for Mary's sake, sing
for the maiden, sing
for God's mother. Sing! (Newman 123)

As these two translations might help us to realize, Hildegard's view
of the incarnation is itself symphonic, harmonizing the apparent
dichotomies of virginity and motherhood, individual and cosmic
parturition, and mysterious impregnation in the past and rapturous ecclesial song in the present. The imagery of generosity and
delight, greenness and fullness, borrowed from the Song of Songs,
here serves a liturgical purpose: the Son and Song of God find a
home in and emanate from Mary's womb (*omnis celestis symphonia de
te sonuit*).

Hildegard continually explores the strength and majesty of
the mother of God. The sequence "*O virga ac diadema*" salutes the
matchless maid as "*auream materiam,*" "a golden vessel" made "out
of his Word" for Grant and "a golden matrix . . . for his word" for
Newman, as "*Aurora,*" whose "new sun came forth from your

womb" and whose "thighs" are "the sunrise," and as "*Salvatrix*,"
"who extended the new light to humanity" and who is herself
"mother of light" (Grant 565; Newman 129–130). In hymns addressed to feminine manifestations of divine power, in Wisdom ("*O
virtus Sapientie*"), the Church ("*O orchzis Ecclesia*"), and Light ("*O
choruscans lux stellarum*"), the emphasis on a force, both nurturant
and regnant, is uppermost. Like *hokmah* in the wisdom literature
(Prov 8:1–21), *Sapientia* for Hildegard encompasses and embraces
all things: "you quicken the world in your clasp" (Newman 101);
Ecclesia is measureless in her circumference, adorned with hya-
cinth and rendered metonymically as "the city of knowledge" (Newman 253); *Lux*, partaking of a special form of regal nuptials, is
bedecked "like a noble lady / without spot or wrinkle" (Newman
255). In commenting on this repertoire of images of the feminine,
Marina Warner deduces that "as Hildegard circles closer and
closer to her own story, of claustration in the Church's service . . .
the virginal body of a woman becomes her dominant symbol, itself
unfolding into a many-petalled cluster of different meanings, emotions, memories and prophecies" (190).

 The *Ordo virtutum,* for which she also composed the music, is
another unfolding, this time in the form of a symphonic and chro-
matically gripping[6] litany of the virtues. Diabolus, the only solo
male voice, is the single speaking part in the otherwise sung play.
As the glorious phrases and closing chant melisma of female voices
stand in contrast to the raspy shrillness of the devil's taunts and
interjections, so the whole exercise underlines the triumph of virtuous artistry and numbers over satanic wiles. In the face of Satan's
promise of immediate rewards and charge that the virtues lack
knowledge of themselves, the Queen Humility makes it clear that,
from her vantage point, "*in excelsis*" (line 67), she is completely
aware of Satan's downcast position "*in abyssum*" (line 66). This
"*gloriosa regina*" and "*suavissima mediatrix*" (line 72), in offering her
followers the skill of finding the lost drachma ("*perditam dragmam,*"
line 70), prompts them to declare themselves after the example of
Charity, whose self-description as "*flos amabilis*" (line 76), flower of
love, initiates a litany of metaphors. Radiant ("*lucida,*" line 88)
Obedience is hailed as "*dulcissima vocatrix*" (line 91), sweetest in-
viter; Faith is calmly mirror-like ("*serena, speculata,*" line 96); and
Hope, the living life and sweet consoler ("*o vivens vita, et o suavis
consolatrix,*" line 101), is also "*dulcis conspectrix*" (line 98), the sweet
beholder. Chastity is particularly self-aware as she apostrophizes
on both virginity and the noble virgin, whom the shadow will never

find in a fading flower ("*o virgo nobilis, te numquam inveniet umbra in cadente flore,*" line 108). The other virtues laud Chastity for remaining in the harmonies of heavenly citizens ("*in symphoniis supernorum civium,*" line 110). It is precisely by this image of concord ("*in symphonia sonare,*" line 194) that the Virtues welcome the fugitive, penitent Soul and lead the attack on Satan for her. Having been given the skill to find the lost coin, the Virtues echo the related Lucan parable (15:4–7) about the lost sheep, "*perditam ovem*" (line 169), in greeting the hesitant Anima.

The symphonic metaphor, which captures "the theme of reintegration of God and his creatures" (Flanagan 140), also reveals Hildegard's "remarkable . . . 'esemplastic power' " (Dronke, *Poetic Individuality,* 177). One feature of Hildegard's ability to shape disparate things into a unified whole is her adroit blending of male and female designations for the virtues/warriors, whom the Soul refers to as the soldiery of the Queen, "*milicia regine*" (line 179), whom Victory exhorts as most brave and glorious soldiers, "*O fortissimi et gloriosissimi milites*" (line 218), and who, themselves, salute Victoria as "*dulcissima bellatrix*" (line 220), sweetest warrior. Another notable way in which Hildegard unifies her play is through the subtle repetition of words. As part of the major declamation of the warriors of Humilitas, while Innocentia, Contemptus Mundi, Amor Celestis, Verecundia, Discretio, and Paciencia describe themselves and praise one another, Misericorida declares the wish to reach out her hand, "*manum porrigere*" (line 138), to all who suffer. Significantly the last word of the play, sung in a chant melisma by a mixed chorus of celebrating virtues and souls, is "*porrigat*"; the singers enjoin their audience to genuflect to God so that He may reach out His hand: "*ut . . . manum suam porrigat*" (line 269). The rich ornamentation of this finale brings an optimistic close to the epilogue's summary of salvation history, in the Edenic beginning of which "*omnes creature viruerunt*" (line 252), all creation was green and flourishing; however, when this greenness faded, a champion, "*vir prelatior*" (line 255), offered his wounds to the Father so that others may also bend their knees to receive divine mercy.

The manuscript illuminations which Hildegard commissioned to accompany her text succeed in translating her revelations, visions, and expostulations through the lavish use of pigments; the cobalt, magenta, vermilion, silver, and gold of the Eibingen manuscript usher the viewer into the complete, corporeal, yet metaphysical, world of her work. The colossal figure of Ecclesia in silver and magenta, for example, with her arms extended in an *orans* gesture, rays of gold framing her face, and a group of nuns and monks at her breast, is actually a visual summation of Hildegard's major themes (Figure 1). The virgin in the foreground of the group of religious imitates the prayerful gesture of the larger figure; although Ecclesia's arms extend to the acanthus border, her eyes search with a real intensity beyond this enclosure. Hildegard's writings could be analogous, in a way, to the foregrounded virgin; their holy and often-biblical inspiration, to the surrounding model of the church.

The visions, which she began to record on divine command in her forty-third year, reflect a wonderful mystic idiosyncracy, as Hildegard turns from one biblical text or episode to another to discuss the origins of the world and the nature of its creatures and creator. Not unlike several contemporaries and predecessors, as Peter Dronke makes clear in *Fabula,* Hildegard envisioned a cosmic egg which she described in detail in the First Part, Third Vision of the *Scivias.* In contrast to other twelfth century cosmologists, however, she stressed the dynamic turbulence within and around this ovoid, encircled by a bright flame with a darker layer under it. There is "a ceaseless interpenetration of creative and destructive forces" (Dronke 97) in Hildegard's vision, as "the fire of the outer edge understood the violence of the sounds of the gloomy fire" (I.iii.1). To bring these dualising images "within the compass of a monistic world-view" (Dronke 99), Hildegard launches a series of allegorical explanations of the shape and contents of this vision. The egg structure, she maintains, "shows faithfully the all-powerful God incomprehensible in majesty and inestimable in divine mysteries and existing as the hope of all the faithful" (I.iii.2). It also reflects the progress of salvation history:

> At first people were untried and simple in their actions, but thereafter those people spread themselves out in the Old and New Testament. Nevertheless around the time of the end of the world all of them may suffer many hardships and difficulties. (I.iii.2)

The visionary is quick to signify God's presence in the bright encircling flame, which indicates "that God burns everywhere through the fire of divine punishment those people who are outside the true faith" (I.iii.3).

Figure 1.
Depiction of *Ecclesia* ("The Church") from Hildegard of Bingen's
Scivias (Eibingen Ms.).

A similar reliance on constructs or figures, such as columns, trees, and human forms, characterizes all of Hildegard's visions. One of her revealing treatments of the wisdom and vigor of the scriptures starts with the sighting of an iron-colored, three-sided column facing east, north, and south, which was "fearful to look at" and surmounted by an indescribably bright light in whose midst appeared a dove holding "a golden ray of light within its mouth" (III.iv.1). The sides of this column are marked either with branches, on which patriarchs and prophets sit, or spaces, where apostles, martyrs, confessors, and virgins walk about "with great joy," or "nubs . . . like the bark of a tree . . . about to sprout." The sword-sharp edges of this column refer, in Hildegard's explication, "to the strength of the Word of God which went around and turned around in grace" (III.iv.5). The nubs manifest "that the Word came between two times—between the time of the patri-archs and prophets and the time of the Word's own teachings" (III.iv.9). The capstone bird enshrined in light points to "the great-est and most profound mystery of the Word . . . in which all justice is brought forth both in laws and in the New Testament—the greatest brightness of shining wisdom" (III.iv.14). Hildegard is often awestruck before the feminine figure of Wisdom. Starting with an image from Sirach of the virtue that was before every creature ("*primogenita ante omnem creaturam,*" Sir 24:5), she pauses in front of this beautiful image, "joined in God and to God in the sweetest embrace in a religious dance of burning love" (III.ix.25), and provides theological interpretations of her vestments (golden tunic and gem-embellished girdle and crown) and posture (with "her hand . . . placed reverently upon her breast" and feet hidden from view). Like all Hildegard's visions, the image is not static, but constantly accumulating symbolic detail:

> Eventually, wisdom was embellished with the whitest vir-ginity of the Virgin Mary, and later with the very strong and ruddy faith of the martyrs. At length she was embel-lished with the purple and bright charity by which God and neighbor ought to be loved through the warmth of the Holy Spirit.

Hildegard's being attuned to the Spirit resulted in images that are at once repetitive and proleptic, grandiose yet difficult to visualize or reconstruct. Although she establishes predictably high, even ideal standards, she never loses sight of the creature in the rapture of her illuminations about the divine. The *De Operatione Dei* praises the symmetry and capacities of the individual's microcosm in light of the surrounding similarities of the universe. Saluting the crown of the human head as "the beginning of the soul's actions" and the reflection of "the roundness of the firmament," Hildegard argues that "God has formed humanity according to the model of the firmament and strengthened human power with the might of the elements" (Vision Four: 16). Her analogies work in both directions, with human anatomy at times prefiguring a universal design.

> The fertile Earth is symbolized by the sex organs, which display the power of generation as well as an indecent boldness. Just as unruly forces at times rise from these organs, the recurring fertility of the Earth brings about a luxuriant growth and an immense overabundance of fruits. (Vision Four: 79)

Motivated though she is toward methods of control and proper use of this plenty, Hildegard, when picturing humanity, impresses me as more compassionate than censorious, willing to believe more in goodness than evil. Her similes describing the blockage of sin are not nearly as developed as the optimistic and ever-associative image clusters surrounding virtue and spiritual power.

> If we fall victim to the burden and excess of our sins, these sins will bunch up within us like a fire that becomes so smothered by dense smoke that it can no longer burn freely. But if carnal desires are driven from the mind by the power of the spirit, we shall burst into sighs of longing for our Father's heavenly home. In a similar way does the bee construct its honeycomb out of its own honey. And thus our new deed and old action are so mingled that they will not burn out or dry up because they are carried out in true humility. (Vision Four: 36)

Rivaling Ezekiel's chariot and Belshazzar's feast for mystery and amplitude, Hildegard's prophetic visions are nevertheless at their core serenely hopeful. The simple image of the honeycomb, emerging, like the sweetness Samson discovered, from the carcass of Hildegard's discussion of sin, affirms the benign and resolute faith of this visionary.

The Nuns of Helfta:
Mechthild of Magdeburg, Mechthild of Hackeborn, and Gertrude the Great

In their daring and passion, their disclosure of individual experience as a meditative norm, the spiritual exercises, litanies, and mystical visions of these thirteenth century nuns herald a new emphasis which distinguishes their interpretive work from earlier material. These women are less concerned with teaching or explicating and more preoccupied with praying and feeling. Boldly and extravagantly personal, they write about encountering and experiencing God in a direct, unmediated fashion. Hence, the Psalms, the Song of Songs, and the New Testament dicta about love are seminal texts in their often-rhapsodic devotions. As Barbara Newman measures the widening distance between scholastic and devotional literature, "many abandoned the sapiential theologians' interest in the epiphanies of God in nature, turning instead to a quest for union with the Unknowable in the depths of the spirit" (258).

But for all the emphasis on interiority and the repeated imagery of the consummated union, it is important, I think, to see their work as much more than rudimentary psychotherapy or mere case studies in self-absorbed eremetism. As well as being a center of learning the convent was a community. Emphasis on the privilege or protection of this enclosure and its distance from the real world of needy and fallible people could lead to the misunderstanding about a monastic elite. The very prodigality of these women's experiences and their explorations of a variety of prayerful modes contribute to the dynamic effects of their solitude and contemplation, making them, in Jean Leclercq's phrase, "a center without circumference." Moreover, Leclercq's claim about the "mystery of solitude and communion" in the "sacrament" of religious life provides a fitting preamble to the intensely self-aware writing of these nuns:

> The monastic person is one who is centered, who *is* the center, who is con-centrated in such a way that in this one person converge as in a single focal point the centers of every other reality. (81)

Mechthild of Magdeburg

Although little is known of Mechthild's life (d. 1282) as a Beguine in Magdeburg, in the last part of her life, when she was blind, she entered the convent at Helfta where she dictated the final section of *Das fliessende Licht der Gottheit* (The Flowing Light of Godhead); these revelations began, according to the Prologue, in 1250. A celebration of the abundant gifts and love of God, Mechthild's writing explores those instances when the soul, separated from the body, is laid "bare to itself" (Section 2) and, in answering the call of "God most glorious," experiences a "two-fold intercourse [in] Love Eternal / Which can never die" (Section 44). Reminiscent of the beloved in the Song of Songs, who is at times the initiator and at times the pursued, Mechthild's soul, as lover and beloved, both longs for consummation and is invited to come to God in the *unio mystica*.

> *Den nim ich, minste sele, in den arm min,*
> *Und isse in und trinke in*
> *Und tun mit im was ich wil.*

> I, the least of souls, will take Him in my arms
> And eat Him and drink Him
> And do with him what I will.

> *Kument ze mitten tage zu dem brunen schatten in das bette der mine, da sont it uch mit im erkulen.*

> Come at midday to the shadow of the spring to the bed
> of love; there you shall cool yourself with Him. (Franklin
> 78, 80)

Such eroticism is typical of her intuitive mysticism. In her role as a simple recorder of the revelations flowing from God, she pictures these revelations again and again in the image of the stream, spring, or brook. Her emphasis on the baptismal significance of water indicates, as James Franklin has argued, a reliance on New Testament models of the transformative, miraculous effects of water (Jn 2:3–10; 5:4; 6:9; 9:6; 13:5; 19:34). While Mechthild sees the Father as "a gushing spring that no one can exhaust" (*ein vsvliessene brune, den nieman erschopfen mag*), she is also aware of the consuming potential when the "*vsvliessende brune*" (gushing spring) changes to "*einn gros himelvlut*" (a great flood); she records this divine greeting:

Min widergrus ist ein so gros himelvlut,
Solte ich mich in dich nach miner maht geben
Du behieltest nit dein mensclich leben.

My greeting in return is a heavenly flood so great
That if I should give Myself to you with all My power
You would lose your mortal life. (Franklin 79)

But she is conscious, too, of the traditional expectations of a predominantly male readership who may not be prepared for divine revelations conveyed by a woman; hence, Mechthild's address to Heinrich of Halle, her first editor, establishes a genuine authorial voice at the same time as it locates her inspired and undeniably learned[7] writing within the company of patriarchs, prophets, and apostles.

> You are surprised at the masculine words which are written in this book. I wonder why that surprises you. But it grieves me more to the heart that I, a sinful woman, must so write. But I cannot describe to anyone the true knowledge and holy, magnificent revelations except with these words alone, which seem to me all too puny in comparison to the eternal truth. I asked the eternal master what he would say about this. And he answered: ask him how it happened that the apostles, when they were first so weak, became so bold after they had received the Holy Spirit. Ask further where Moses was when he saw only God. Ask yet further how it was that Daniel spoke in his childhood. (Howard 168)

Mechthild of Hackeborn

Mechthild of Hackeborn (1241–1299) entered the convent at the age of seven and spent much of her adult life as a kind of administrative assistant to her sister, Gertrude, who was the abbess at Helfta. Mechthild was mistress of novices and choir director; because of reports of the sweetness of her voice, she has been called the "Nightingale of the Lord" (Halligan 36). Her mystical text is the *Liber Spiritualis Gratiae*, translated into English by a fifteenth century monk as *The Booke of Gostlye Grace*. Its measured equanimity of tone is a clear indication of its thesis: that for this nun observance of the monastic hours, reception of the sacraments, and attendance at liturgies provide opportunities for illuminating conversations with God as preludes to the heavenly spousal.

The celebration of an Easter liturgy, for example, prompts Mechthild to contemplate the divine life within her; the Lord talks to her at communion on, in his words, this question: " 'Whilte thowe see nowe howe I am in thee, ande thow in me?' " (166–167). Her interlocutor cites Pauline precedent to enhance her sense of humility and dependence:

> Bethenke thee ande haffe mynde of that Poule wrytes ande says of hymselfe: Ego sum minimus apostolorum, that es to saye: I am the leest of apostylys whiche am nowght worthye to be calledde apostle. Be the grace of God I am that I am. Ryght so thou erte nowght in thee, botte that same that thowe erte, be my grace thowe erte in me.

One feature of the Easter liturgy itself, described as burying the cross in the sepulcher, provides a succinct summary of the divine presence in this promise: " 'I will burrye me in thee.' " The hours sung at matins, prime, sext, none, and compline supply, according to Mechthild's divine mentor, a series of meditations on the passion, crucifixion, and resurrection. She is, first of all, to think of her loving Lord "bownde into the handdis of wikkede mene" (469–470). His suffering and ignominious treatment are to be "the sugett in thy herte," preparing her to imitate by performing "alle fylthes and alle lowlye seruyces." In contemplating her lover "festenedde to the crosse," Mechthild herself is to be "crucyfiedde to the worlde." Although she is directed to "dye to the worlde ande to eche creature," she closes the day with the thought of Christ being taken down off the cross—the analogous hope being to be comforted "in [His] lappe with a blessede reste"—and forecasts of the blissful union "wharein thowe schalte be mayde oo [one] spyritte with me . . . [in] a blysse endurynge ande abydynge withowten eende."

Gertrude the Great

During the tenure of Gertrude of Hackeborn as abbess, another visionary, Gertrude the Great (1256–1302), lived in the convent at Helfta. Gertrude's seven-part *Exercitia* also pivots around sacramental and liturgical celebrations, such as baptism, the taking of the habit, and pronouncement of vows. But, unlike Mechthild's work, Gertrude's writing is full of rhapsodic surprises: this chantress, on occasion, assumes the roles of poet, instrumentalist, and symphonic conductor (Hourlier 50). Her first-person voice is much more daring and audible than the remote and cautiously disquieting third-person style of Mechthild of Hackeborn.

Since a modern English translation of one of Gertrude's litanies of praise, the Mystical *Jubilus*, from the *Exercises* is already available,[8] I think a sampling of two different forms, the petition and the benediction, might underscore the personal immediacy and celebratory audacity of her writing. Calling on Jesus, for mercy's sake (*Eia Iesu*), and asking, like the psalmist (70/71:8), to have her mouth full of your praise (*tu reple os meum laude tua*), she addresses her Lord as the wisest worker (*operator sapientissime*), the most excellent artist (*artifex praestantissime*), her refuge and strength (*refugium meum et virtus*), and her beloved (*dilecte mi*) (VII. 637–42; Hourlier 302). Suitably this catalogue of petitioning metaphors and biblical symbols climaxes in her invocation, inspired by the Song of Songs (5:10), of her legitimate spouse chosen out of a thousand (*legitimus sponsus meus electus ex millibus*), in whose tender embraces she wants to exult (*in praedulces amplexus tuos ruam sine mora*). The way in which Gertrude works so many biblical texts and echoes into the fabric of her petition shows her intimate familiarity with the Vulgate. The Bible provides, in every sense of the word, the ground of her prayers. As a pilgrim speaking to her protector (*o fidele praesidium itineris mei*), she recalls the psalmist (41:5/ 43:3–4) entering joyously the area of the tabernacle as far as the house of the Lord (*laetabunda ingradiar locum tabernaculi admirabilis usque ad domum dei*), and borrows from the first letter to the Corinthians (9:24) the image of running the race to win the prize (*quia tu es unicum meum, pro quo curro, bravium*). Similarly apposite is her petitioning of the Lord of her life (*Eia o deus vitae meae*) as a prelude to her supplication that, in a fashion reminiscent of the blooming of the new Jerusalem at the close of Isaiah's vision (65:19–25), she herself might experience new life, reflower, and gain the strength to produce worthy fruits (*in te revireat, refloreat, et in fructos dignos convalescat vita mea*). The final benediction of the *Exercises* captures for me Gertrude's essential joy not only in being part of the Lord but in being transformed by that fact as well. With a voice that is confident rather than plangent, she seeks a blessing that will confirm her purpose as a humble subject desiring the perfection of unity with her Lord:

Benedicat mihi obsecro hodie, Iesu chare, anima tua. Benedicat mihi imperialis divinitas tua. Benedicat mihi fructosa humanitas tua in tanta efficacia, ut tua regalis munificentia mihi reliquat tuae benedictionis signa tam evidentia quatenus a me tota permutata, in te amore invincibili, inseparabiliter tibi adhaeream. Fac me in tuo timore perfectam. (Hourlier 306)

May your spirit this day, sweet Jesus, bless me, I beseech you. May your imperial divinity bless me. May your humanity so rich in fruits bless me, with such an efficacity that your royal generosity leaves in me evident signs of your blessing; so that transformed from myself into you by an unbeatable love, I will cling totally to you. Make me perfect in your love.

New Forms of Piety:
Hadewijch of Brabant and Catherine of Siena

In addition to being rich periods for mystical writing, the thirteenth and fourteenth centuries were also chaotic times for the church, when the susceptibility of established forms to corruption and abuse was manifest. The voices of female mystics, suggesting a return to true apostolic life and acknowledging the facts of pain and worldly rejection in the pursuit of the love of God, were strong influences in support of reform and such new religious groups as Beguinages and mendicant orders. Rather than stressing the spontaneous emergence of the Beguines, Carol Neel's recent study seeks to uncover their possible antecedents in the mystical piety of Cistercian and Premonstratensian orders. "While early beguine life trangressed the boundary between laypersons and religious in an especially obvious fashion," Neel argues, "that boundary had for a hundred years been eroded by the participation of lay brothers as well as lay sisters in reformed monasticism" (337). The zealous renunciation of comfort and security was directly proportional to the desire of Beguines and mendicants to live and die with Christ. The Bible in general afforded them models and signposts for following this unitive life.

The Beguine Hadewijch of Brabant

The austere communities of religious women, the Beguines, who took no formal vows and devoted themselves to prayer and charitable service, are best represented in the works of the thirteenth century Brabant mystic, Hadewijch. Although scarcely anything is known of her life itself, aside from deductions about her aristocratic past, a period as mistress of a Beguine group, and final service in a hospital for the poor, her visions, letters, and poems, among the early masterworks of Dutch literature, reveal a great deal about the nature of the mystical experience. Propelled by an intense devotion to *Minne* (love), Hadewijch's writings on the one hand show the attraction of the fruitive being-one aspect of mysticism, and on the other dare to talk about the demystifying, human, sensual experience. In cataloguing "women-identified women in medieval Christianity," Ann Matter focuses on the concept of *Minne,* a blending of powerfully divine and "intimately human" (85) love, as the basis of her suggestion (unconvincing, in my estimate) of "a possible interpretation" that Hadewijch and another Beguine were "particular" (86) lesbian friends. The end of mysticism, however, is never worldly, physical, or sexual gratification, but the discovery of "the price of Love in misery" (Poem 27), the realization that "Consolation and ill-treatment, both at once,/ [Are] the essence of the taste of Love" (Poem 31).

I have chosen Hadewijch's "The Jacob Letter" (Letter 12) to illustrate some of these general themes. It opens with a double wish, which is also a mystical covenant: "May God be God for you, and may you be love for him!" The model of love, originating in humility, is Mary, the "loveress," who, in Hadewijch's allusion to the Magnificat (Lk 1:46–55), "drew him into herself." The ideal is to remain "unassuming in all things and unconquered by any kind of service." It may appear a form of negative capability to be so empty of self, so vigilant about losing direction; yet this is precisely the way, Hadewijch maintains, to "begin here on earth that eternal life by which God lives eternally." The element of imperfectibility in these yearnings is nevertheless strong; referring obliquely to the Johannine pericope about God being love (I Jn 4:16), Hadewijch warns that "the sublime Love, indeed, and the grandeur that is God are never satisfied or known by all that man can accomplish." This attachment to the mystery of the unknowable God establishes the first of the many binary opposites of this letter. In contrast to those who, in their desire "to content Love, are also eternal and unfathomable" stand the "low-minded . . . who are not enthralled by eternal Love." She cites Paul's characterization (1 Cor 1:9) of God as "true fidelity" in exhorting her reader to enjoy this "mutual interpenetration . . . [this] blissful fruition . . . flowing into his goodness and flowing out again in all good." The knowledge of the presence of woe in bliss leads to her second set of opposites, which recall Matthew's distinctions (7:13–14): against the "emotional attraction of worldly joy . . . [and] frivolous love" are the straight and narrow ways to "sublime Love."

Hadewijch's peroration starts with a slow drum roll of allusions to the Old and New Testament injunctions to love the Lord with heart, soul, and mind (Mt 22:37; Mk 12:30; Lk 10:27): "He gave this commandment to Moses and in the Gospel, that in this way we should live wholly for Love." Her extended example, however, comes not from an evangelist, but from Obadiah, the shortest of the prophetic books, forewarning the downfall of Edom and predicting the restoration of Judah. She does not emphasize imprecations but rather concentrates on promises of success to those who have wrestled with the Lord and limped away with a blessing.

> Consider also what Obadiah the prophet says: *The house of Jacob shall be a fire; the house of Joseph shall be a flame; the house of Esau shall be stubble.* Jacob is everyone who conquers; by the power of love, he conquered God, in order to be conquered himself. . . . Whoever wishes to wrestle with God must set himself to conquer in order to be conquered; and he must start to limp on the side on which there is anything else for him besides God alone, or on which anything else is dearer than God.

She interprets the flame of Joseph as another type of saving leadership. But what is most peculiar about Hadewijch's exegesis is her treatment of the house of Esau reduced to stubble. The obliteration of the house of Esau as a morally motivated act of providence is part of the prophet's overall threat of disaster: "they shall burn them and consume them, and there shall be no survivor to the house of Esau, for the Lord has spoken" (18b). In the mystic's letter, however, the house of Esau serves to challenge the dedication, the true flame, of exemplars and reformers in lay and religious life.

> The aliens among the common people are Esau. Their
> house is stubble, which is rapidly ignited by fiery flames;
> so shall the others be ignited by you, when you are a
> flame. This pertains to your function of prelacy in the
> monastery: that you kindle the dry stubble by your good
> example, by your way of life, and by your commands,
> counsels, and admonitions.

Her farewell, "Make haste to love," aptly summarizes Hadewijch's
own life, "one of devotion to God in a search for spiritual perfection within the lay world" (Devlin 193).

The Dominican Catherine of Siena

In her short life Catherine of Siena (1347–1380) was on the
same quest. Yet this Dominican tertiary was also embroiled in the
murderous quarrels between Guelph and Ghibelline factions and
in ultimately abortive attempts to restore peace between the city-
state of Florence and Rome. Her mystical treatise, the *Dialogo* (The
Dialogue), does not deny the reality of suffering which, for those
who have united themselves to Christ, is "a delight"; pleasure, for
them, "is wearisome, as is every consolation or delight the world
may offer" (Noffke 44). In fact, suffering becomes "the fundamental symbol of humanity's separation from God" (Costello 56). Catherine's conversation with the creator-redeemer-Spirit is a series of
extended symbols explained in the process of her earnest questions, the lengthy divine replies, and her prayerful thanks. One of
the central symbols is of Christ as the bridge and, fittingly, the
major biblical source quoted directly throughout Christ's speeches
is the gospel of John, from which notions of a sustaining link could
clearly have been deduced if not derived. Life-giving Johannine
symbols of water, bread, temple, and light permeate Catherine's
text. On the overall influence of the Bible in *The Dialogue*, Catherine's most recent translator, Suzanne Noffke, has commented:

> The Scriptures she heard and read presumably only in
> Latin are at home in her works, in her own dialect, with a
> natural sort of familiarity that is strongly reminiscent of
> the long savoring and fondling of the old Jewish masters.
> These are no mere recited "proof texts." They flow in
> and out of her sentences with such ease and integration
> that it is more often than not difficult to set them off with

quotation marks. She so rearranges and combines passages around a single stream of thought that her own message and that of the Scriptures fuse into one. (10)

This fusion is especially apparent in the responses of "God eternal" about the redemptive bridge created by his Son's sacrifice.

> Nor could anyone walk on that bridge until my Son was raised up. This is why he said, "If I am lifted up high I will draw everything to myself." . . . In this way he drew everything to himself: for he proved his unspeakable love, and the human heart is always drawn by love. He could not have shown you greater love than by giving his life for you. You can hardly resist being drawn by love, then, unless you foolishly refuse to be drawn. (65)

The divine explanations of this structure "joining the most high with the most lowly" (68) are at times more oblique renderings of biblical imagery. Although allusions to the building metaphor of 1 Peter 2 are discernible, Catherine's rearrangement and integration of various passages have the effect of creating an utterly distinct spiritual construct. Opening the heavens "with the key of his blood," sheltering pilgrims with a covering over the bridge in the form of "walls and a roof of mercy," and building with basic materials of "living stones" are among the more puzzling images with layered meanings used by the divine speaker.

> By my power the stones of virtue were built into walls on no less a foundation than himself, for all virtue draws life from him, nor is there any virtue that has not been tested in him. So no one can have any life-giving virtue but from him, that is, by following his example and his teaching. He perfected the virtues and planted them as living stones built into walls with his blood. So now all the faithful can walk without hindrance and with no cringing fear of the rain of divine justice, because they are sheltered by the mercy that came down from heaven through the incarnation of this Son of mine. (66)

In Catherine's text apocalyptic allusions are prominent (Rev 19:11–13; 21:18–20), and analogues are never singular. Just as blood can be both mortar and key, the virtues are divine gifts and living stones—with such doubleness emphasizing the mysteries and para-doxes of gift-giving and animation.

Related to the multi-valences of her imagery are the central dualities separating earth from heaven, physicality from spiritual-ity, and the body which for Catherine is the mere "garment of selfish sensuality" (141) from the soul which is searching for a "goal [that] is not this life" (100). The major paradox of Cather-ine's writing is that it stresses mortification and eschews the sensual and the worldly in a style remarkable for its bodily fervor and torrential emotion.

Margery Kempe and Julian of Norwich

The rejection of the body is not nearly as strong a motif in the life story Margery Kempe (1373–c.1438) dictated or the series of revelations Julian of Norwich (1343–1416) described. In fact, *The Book of Margery Kempe* and Julian's *Showings* both emphasize the body as a means of experiencing and a model for relaying the mysteries of divine love. While the majestic power of this love often causes Margery literally to lose strength and fall down, this same power, figuring the parental concern of God the Father and God the Mother, is the source of Julian's buoyant and sustaining hope. Through direct quotation and less direct allusion in their writing, the Bible supported these mystics with affirmations of their unique gifts and blessings.

Margery Kempe

The first autobiography in English, *The Book of Margery Kempe* is also the first instance where an author consciously grapples with the issues of female spirituality and selfhood (Mueller 155). Mar-gery's struggle as a recorder of events dictated to a scribe reflects the larger anomaly of the claim of this woman, who was the wife of a burgess of Lynn and mother of fourteen children, to a mystical spousal as the bride of Christ. She is capable of presenting herself as a prophet without honor in her own country and even a teacher in the temple. Her energy and candor in making her life the book of spiritual instruction result in extraordinarily touching revela-tions, especially about the taunts and pains she endured.

The occasion of her interview (chapter 17) with the vicar of St. Stephen's in Norwich furnishes an example of the ways in which Margery lived by, and through her presence challenged others to attend to, the redemptive ethos of the New Testament. At times Margery impresses the reader as deliberate and self-conscious in her Christian propagandism; at others, she appears almost ingenuous, unwittingly affecting those around her. When the vicar greets her decidedly humble request "to speak . . . for an hour or two, in the afternoon when he had eaten, about the love of God" with barely disguised patronage—"Bless us! How could a woman occupy one or two hours with the love of our Lord? I shan't eat a thing till I find out what you can say of our Lord God in the space of an hour"—Margery does not shrink, but immediately launches into a candid confession of her shortcomings.

> Afterwards she told him the whole manner of her life from her childhood, as closely as it would come to mind— how unkind and unnatural she had been towards our Lord Jesus Christ; how proud and vain she had been in her bearing; how obstinate against the laws of God, and how envious towards her fellow Christians; how she was chastized (later when it pleased our Lord Jesus Christ) with many tribulations and horrible temptations, and how afterwards she was fed and comforted with holy meditations, and especially in the memory of our Lord's Passion. (Windeatt 74)

Her recital is general enough to prompt a reaction about the inadvisability of judging others (Mt 7:1), and yet suffused with such faith in Christ crucified (Rom 6:8) that the listener might also be left in a little awe. Although Margery suffers a loss of bodily strength as a result of her thoughts about the passion, her faith is actually the source of great robustness and joy (cf. Rom 5:22).

So direct and personal an experience is Margery's faith, so superior to mere book learning or to the meditations of others, that she speaks with complete openness about her friendship with the Trinity, the sense of connectedness she feels to the mystical tradition of Walter Hilton, Saint Bridget, and Richard Rolle, and her attachment to the communion of apostles, saints, and martyrs:

> She told him how sometimes the Father of heaven conversed with her soul as plainly and as certainly as one friend speaks to another through bodily speech . . . sometimes all Three Persons in the Trinity and one substance in Godhead spoke to her soul and informed her in faith

and in his love—how she should love him, worship him, and dread him—so excellently that she heard never a book, neither Hilton's book, nor Bride's [Bridget's] book, nor *Stimulus Amoris,* not *Incendium Amoris,* nor any other book that ever she heard read, that spoke so exaltedly of the love of God as she felt highly working of her soul, if she could have communicated what she felt. Sometimes our Lady spoke to her mind. Sometimes Saint Peter, sometimes Saint Paul, sometimes Saint Katherine, or whatever saint in heaven she was devoted to, appeared to her soul and taught her how she should love our Lord and how she should please him. (75)

Margery not only documents her travels to religious centers throughout England to speak to episcopal leaders like the bishop of Lincoln and the archbishop of Canterbury; she also records her considerable travel to shrines in Jerusalem, Rome, and Santiago. Often berated, ridiculed, misunderstood, and, in her long journeys, ostracized because of her ignorance of the native languages, Margery remains attached to and confident in her highly personalized, emotional faith. Her comments on the Passiontide liturgies (chapters 79–81), so effusive and immediate in their composition of place, so blithe in introducing Margery herself as the companion of Mary the mother of God and Mary Magdalene, capture the essential characteristic of this interpreter as an empathetic narrator who puts herself and her reader into the biblical account. "As freshly and veritably as if they had been done in her bodily sight," she weeps along with Mary as Jesus' accusers "lug his blessed ears and pull the hair of his beard" (chapter 79). She is more than an observer during the scourging when she cries out "Kill me instead, and let him go" (chapter 80). Yet despite her sense of participation in these accounts, Margery is acutely aware of the humbling divide between herself and her creator; the words "touch me not" set off another burst of tears on account of "the love and desire that she had to be with our Lord" (chapter 81).

In *The Later Middle Ages* Stephen Medcalf quotes the "modern diagnosis" (114) of Dr. Anthony Ryle, who conducts a psychoanalytic examination of Margery; in her behavior Ryle detects attention-seeking strategies and hysterical personality traits. In a women's studies course this year, devoted to medieval and renaissance women writers, I assigned an essay topic involving an assessment of Ryle's diagnosis. It had been hard to pry the students—mainly seniors and a few graduate students—away from Margery's *Book*. They loved the confessional frankness, her acknowledgement of sexual temptation, her shrewdness in detecting which clerics were trustworthy and which were scoundrels, and sympathized fully with her sense of loneliness and isolation. Margery's human features, in a sense, sold her theological message; even unchurched and agnostic students were volunteering biblical allusions to buttress the validity of Margery's claims. Ryle's diagnosis, I'll admit, did not stand much of a chance! Most who chose the topic had an anachronistic field day with the anti-psychiatric thesis. The more searching papers weighed the awkward, involuntary, seizure-like aspects of Margery's declarations of faith and atonement against the openness of her other disclosures about vanity and sexuality and the rebukes she tolerated; they concluded in favor of the unhysterical but not merely self-serving honesty of Margery's dictation.

An equally revealing assessment of Margery emerges from comparing her to contemporary and earlier religious women; such a treatment also emphasizes her uniqueness. Unlike the divine directives which led Mechthild of Hackeborn in her liturgically focused meditations on the passion and resurrection, Margery creates her own scenic color and affecting drama. Moreover, unlike the serene faith of her immured contemporary Julian, a faith in many ways symbolized by withdrawal to the cell of the soul, Margery felt the constant need to display, test, and confirm her belief in a public forum.

Julian of Norwich

One advisor to whom Margery had recourse was the anchoress who lived enclosed in a cell adjoining the parish church of St. Julian in Conisford at Norwich. Given the amplitude, vigor, and discernment of Julian's writing, it is difficult to imagine her enclosure in the whimsical simile of Sylvia Townsend Warner as "a cell, fastened like a moth's coffin, to the side of some church" (*The Corner That Held Them*, 158). With no defensiveness, no trace of rationalizing the female voice or experience, the short and long texts of Julian's *Showings* illustrate how well-equipped she was for the roles of counselor and interpreter. Combining the deft art of rhetorical simplicity and a thorough grounding in scripture she uses accounts of her own infirmity as a way of talking about God the servant; her explanation

of the servant's complementary motherhood and fatherhood provide, in my estimate, the most provocative and curiously modern
statement of medieval female spirituality.

As is so often the case with these women for whom exegesis
consisted of spontaneous incorporation of biblical texts and allusions in their descriptions of visionary experiences, the Bible is the
prime influence on the style and symbology of Julian's accounts of
the revelations she was granted. The most prominent texts concern the Pauline doctrine of soteriology, in which Christ sent "his
own Son in the likeness of sinful flesh, and for sin, he condemned
sin in the flesh" (Rom 8:3), making us "fellow heirs with Christ"
(Rom 8:17) to be glorified together with him. As Paul maintains
that "the sufferings of this present time are not worth comparing
with the glory that is to be revealed to us" (Rom 8:18), so Julian
relates that "all souls who will be saved escape him [the fiend] to
God's glory by the power of our Lord's precious Passion" (Colledge and Walsh 201); the vision even prompts Julian to laugh,
"for I understood that we may laugh, to comfort ourselves and
rejoice in God, because the devil is overcome" (202).

The passion is for this mystic both a restorative sight and a
salvific, shared experience. Echoing Paul's teaching of the triumph
of grace over sin—"As sin reigned in death, grace also might reign
through righteousness to eternal life through Jesus Christ our
Lord" (Rom 5:21)—and the human reality of groaning "in travail
together" (Rom 8:22), Julian writes of the strength and sympathetic assurance she has gained through visions of the passion.

> With this sight of his blessed Passion, with the divinity
> which I saw in my understanding, I knew well that this was
> strength enough for me, yes, and for all living creatures
> who were to be saved, against all the devils of hell and
> against all their spiritual enemies. (Chapter Four, 182)

> Here I saw a great unity between Christ and us, as I
> understand it; for when he was in pain we were in pain,
> and all creatures able to suffer pain suffered with him.
> (Chapter Eighteen, 210)

She derives the most comfort, however, from meditating on
the tenderness, compassion, and pity of the Lord for his beloved,
loyal, and persevering servant. Since both Adam and the Son are
figures of the servant, the christological dimension of suffering

becomes a repeated theme. Yet her related emphasis on the compassionate nurturance of God makes the motif of God as Mother equally strong and reiterated. Julian's exploration of the motherhood of God, in Her active, prescient, loving involvement with mankind, has inspired many contemporary feminist theologians in their work of reclaiming the biblical imagery of the feminine divine. What is most exciting for me are the ease and confidence with which Julian compresses the aspects of our Mother "in nature," "in grace," and "in all things" by alluding to, without ever specifying, the protective refuge of Yahweh's wings (Ps 61:4), the maternal guide whom Moses implores (Num 11:12–13), the living font (Jer 2:13), or the brooding hen (Mt 23:37).

> And so Jesus is our true Mother in nature by our first creation, and he is our true Mother in grace by his taking our created nature. All the lovely works and all the sweet loving offices of beloved motherhood are appropriated to the second person, for in him we have this godly will, whole and safe forever, both in nature and in grace, from his own goodness proper to him.
>
> I understand three ways of contemplating motherhood in God. The first is the foundation of our nature's creation; the second is his taking of our nature, where the motherhood of grace begins; the third is the motherhood at work. And in that, by the same grace, everything is penetrated, in length and in breadth, in height and in depth without end; and it is all one love. (Chapter Fifty-Nine, 296–297)

Here is an ideal instance of the combination of the individual and the collective in the act of interpretation. The personal aspect of divine motherhood, joining triune grace, loving offices, and godly will, arises for this celibate woman not from her own experience, but rather from the belief which links her to a larger though unseen community. The itemizing and logical ordering of her showings, so unlike Margery's enthusiastic outbursts, testifies nonetheless to a shared faith. Julian's style, less performative and more analytic than Margery's, aims in its unique way at reaching out and embracing with a unifying love. Her image of "motherhood at work" is at once personal and universal, theological and practical, divine and human.

3

Renaissance Exegetes: Dissidence and Protestant Mysticism

Oh it is Lord, then sweet surely
   to read of such things here,
And *John* he mourn'd abundantly,
   that th' mystery might draw near,
That new Jersualem above
   might come down here below,
And that they might see their High,
   when that forth he doth go.
              —Anna Trapnel, *The Cry of a Stone*

Many can speak well, but few can do well. We are better scholars in the theory than in the practic part, but he is a true Christian that is a proficient in both.
              —Anne Bradstreet, *Meditations Divine and Moral*

The Eternal Word did open itself thus in me, how that the Spirit from the Word of Life, had at sundry times, and diversely by Vision and Prophecy been opening the Mystery of Faith unto me, for the end that I might a skilful Practitioner in it come to be, and now again a *Live Coal* was put into my Hand with an inspiring Breath that I did feel as Wind did blow upon it while I held it in my hand, so as that many sparks were blown from it.
              —Jane Lead, *The Tree of Faith*

Rembrandt's painting called Old Woman Reading (*Lezende Oude Vrouw*, 1655) is for me an evocative introduction to the renaissance figures. It depicts the upper torso of a seated woman whose hands are clasping a book on which her eyes are riveted. Wisps of

72

white hair are visible beneath her hooded cape; the eye sockets, though sunken, emphasize the roundness of the down-turned lids and the absorption of the gaze. The slightly parted lips suggest that she could be reciting or perhaps simply assenting to the material on the page. There is no background to speak of. The compelling feature is the way in which Rembrandt has allowed the only light in the painting to appear to arise from the book itself. It illuminates the sharply featured face and accounts for the blended mood of serenity and fixity. Although the lives of the three women on whom this chapter will concentrate were not serene, their unswerving determination to read and speak for themselves promotes the fanciful suggestion that any one of them could have served as Rembrandt's model.

If an aural analogue as well might put these figures in some perspective, the dilemmas they faced because of their interpretive work suggest a curious kinship with such a character as Carlo Ginzburg's miller of Friuli who, in *The Worm and the Cheese* (1976), is interrogated for owning a vernacular Bible. The timbre of the impassioned reformers, facing entrenched and authoritative ecclesial opposition, actually deflects as much attention on their accusers. The voices of judgment are absolute and intransigent, whether condemning sexual misconduct, as Judith Brown has sketched its consequences in *Immodest Acts: The Life of a Lesbian Nun in Renaissance Italy*, sifting claims of visions and visitations for proof of demonic possession or fraud, or reiterating doctrine in the face of what seems recalcitrant, impudent negation.

Both Marie Dentière, an ex-Augustinian nun who together with her husband promoted evangelization in the city-state of Geneva, and Anne Askew, the Smithfield martyr who refused to accept the doctrine of transubstantiation, were as dedicated to reform as Hadewijch of Brabant or Catherine of Siena. Yet the polemical activity of these sixteenth century women resulted in much harsher consequences than those endured by the medieval mystics, who can only generally be understood as their counterparts. Whereas Hadewijch and Catherine worked within the confines of the magisterium, Marie Dentière and Anne Askew consciously challenged and refused these limitations; they were also defending women's rights to interpret and disagree with accepted doctrine, both Catholic and Protestant, at a time when reform and counter-reform movements had already effected an increased authoritarianism, hierarchicalism, and certainty within the clerical ranks. The visionary closing this section, Jane Lead (1624–1704), who was a disciple of Jacob

Boehme and promoter of the short-lived Philadelphian movement in late seventeenth century England, provides a baroque coda to most of the medieval and renaissance works as a whole. Prophetess and theosophist, she was preoccupied with the mystical veneration of the Virgin-Sophia or Wisdom; her idiosyncratic borrowings and alterations of biblical stories and figures not only clarify the distinctiveness of her Behmenistic teaching but also serve as contrasts to the visions and female manifestations of divinity in Hildegard of Bingen, thereby pointing to the turns and twists in the development of women's interpretive work over this long period.

Marie Dentière

Marie Dentière's two extant tracts, *La guerre et délivrance de la ville de Génèsve* (The War for and Deliverance of the City of Geneva) and *Epistre très utile, faicte et composée par une femme chréstienne de Tornay* (A Very Useful Letter, Prepared and Written by a Christian Woman of Tournai), show how capable she was in assembling biblical precedents to support her claims about God's intervention in seemingly hopeless cases, to defend the bravery and capabilities of women, and to inveigh against religious hypocrisy. In 1536 she wrote the tract about Geneva in the guise of an anonymous merchant, but three years later she boldly proclaimed her gender and disclosed her initials on the title page of her epistle to the queen of Navarre, the king's sister. Although the tradition persisted of attributing this epistle to Dentière's second husband, the reformer Antoine Froment, despite his declarations that it was not his work, the nineteenth century editor of the correspondence of these reformers, Aimé-Louis Herminjard, has concluded that the epistle's style is superior to that of Froment: "*il est plus vif, plus alerte, plus direct et ne trahit jamais chez l'écrivain la moindre hésitation*" (it is more lively, discerning and direct, never betraying the least hestitation on the part of the author) (V: 304). It is also clearly provocative writing, designed to inform the queen of Dentière's sense of sisterhood with the biblical women of strength and faith at the same time as it opens an unequivocal attack on the clerical hierarchy.

Praising the deeds and example of famous and forgotten biblical women—from Sarah, Rebecca, the queen of Sheba, the Virgin Mary, Elizabeth, and Mary Magdalene to the mother of Moses and the Samaritan woman—fortifies her case for the importance of women's instructing one another, especially at the present, when errors and false doctrines are so rife; "*la terre est remplie de malédic-*

tion" (the world is full of cursing), she observes. It is just as imperative, in Dentière's view, for women to be informed as for men:

> *Car ce que Dieu vous a donné, et à nous femmes révélé, non plus*
> *que les hommes le debvons cacher et fouyr dedens la terre. Et*
> *combien que [ne] nous soit permiz de prêscher es assemblées et*
> *églises publiques, ce néantmoins n'est pas déffendu d'éscrire et*
> *admonester l'une l'aultre, en toute charité.*

> For women, no more than men, should not bury in the
> earth what God has revealed to us. And even though we
> are not permitted to preach in assemblies and public
> churches, we may nevertheless write to and advise one
> another in all charity.

Although she presents herself as a believer held in captivity, like
others driven from their countries, parents, and friends (*"déchas-
sées de leur pays, parans et amys, comme moy"*) on account of the word
of God (*"pour la parolle de Dieu"*), she is no penitent seeking for
reentrance to Romish security. Instead she shows her colors as a
polemical exegete. Like a wisdom writer, she announces herself as
an opponent of prevailing stultification. *"Celuy qui chemine en
ténèbres hayt la lumière: qui a bon droict, il le montre"* (the person who
walks in darkness hates the light; the one who is in the right shows
it). Against false prophets and sycophantic, tyrannical clergymen,
Dentière upholds the example of Jesus. *"Jésus est véritable en ses
promesses, il ne ment pas comme les aultres hommes"* (Jesus is genuine in
his promises; he does not lie like other men). Her attack is vitriolic,
making no bones about the mercenary clerics who are as odious as
vermin (*"telle vermine sur terre"*) and daring as slugs (*"hardis comme
limaces"*) in their campaigns to acquire a bishopric (*"crocheter un
évèsché"*) and satisfy their bellies (*"pour bien sçavoir paistre leur
ventre"*). In the midst of her catalogue of asses, wolves and libidi-
nous cockroaches (*"telz asnes, loups et impudens libins cafardz"*), she
establishes her position as a member of the truly loyal opposition
by aligning herself with two powerful figures: the apostle Paul and
the prophet Isaiah. Although the plotting and abuse she exposes
impress her as a fulfillment of Isaiah's prophecy, *"Ils sont retournez
en leur voye, chascun à son avarice de son costé"*: they have returned in
their way, each to the avarice of his side (possibly based on 56:11),
the prophet's repeated call (10:21; 35:10; 44:22; 63:17) for a return to forgiveness and redemption is the more positive direction

which she chooses not to emphasize. However, Dentière does take heart from the example of the apostle's perseverance with the backsliding community of Galatia. Against the Galatians' return to abolished Mosaic ceremonies, Paul upheld the equality of all believers under the new dispensation, a position which Dentière uses to focus her argument against clerical abuses:

> *A l'imitation duquel apostre doibvent cheminer tous prêscheurs et ministres de la Parolle de Dieu, ne regardans aultre chose sinon que Dieu soit glorifié et honoré par toute la terre, et le prochain gaigné à nostre Seigneur.*

> In imitation of that apostle all preachers and ministers of the word of God should proceed, not worrying about anything else except that God be glorified and honored throughout this world and that they be joined to the saviour in the next.

The sentence which follows this call for Pauline imitation is a shrewd commentary on its high ideals and a recognition of the need for constant vigilance in sifting true from false apostles.

> *Mais il fault que Judas soit avec Christ.*

> But it was necessary that Judas be with Christ.

Anne Askew

Seven years after this epistle, when Anne Askew stood condemned before a clerical tribunal at Sadlers' Hall and later before the King's Council at Greenwich for refusing to believe in transubstantiation, she must have felt an antipathy toward the church hierarchy similar to that expressed by her Genevan forerunner. The time was the last year of the reign of Henry VIII who, though he had progressed in little more than a decade from being declared *Defensor Fidei* to declaring himself the head of the English church, and though he had dissolved and suppressed monasteries, still abided by many Roman doctrines.[1] For Henry's officials, Askew was obstinate and transgressive. The extant partisan report of her trial, *The Account of the Sufferings of Anne Askew, For Opposing the Gross Fiction of Transubstantiation, which is so repugnant to truth and common sense, and has no warrant whatever from Scripture*, is the work of the ex-Carmelite friar and avowed "anti-papist," John Bale; it is a collection of Askew's reported words and her advocate's vituperative commentary. Tendentious though it is, *The Account* illustrates Askew's ability to cite scripture in her own defense and to articulate unflinchingly her dissatisfaction with liturgical practices and eucharistic beliefs. In studying the testimony of Askew, Elaine Beilin concludes that as this defendant "moved from reading and knowing the Bible to quoting it in public and writing it down in the context of her own story, she was breaking down prohibitions against women that had stood for centuries" (47).

Aquinas had defined transubstantiation in the *Summa Theologica* as the change of "the whole substance of the bread . . . into the whole substance of Christ's body, and the whole substance of the wine into the whole substance of Christ's blood" (3a, 75.4). Furthermore, the Council of Florence in 1439 had explained the teaching as authoritative, and the Council of Trent would later promulgate it as part of "the conviction of the church of God" (11 October 1551). Yet Askew denied the doctrine flatly. She even refused the Lutheran idea of consubstantiation, whereby Christ's human nature co-exists with other created objects, in her insistence that the host was only "a piece of bread":

> For a mere proof thereof (mark it when you list), let it but lie in the box three months, and it will be mouldy, and so turn to nothing that is good. Whereupon I am persuaded that it cannot be God. (37–38)

The interrogators bring about no wavering in this defendant; on the contrary, she feels prompted to cite biblical incidents of the worship of false gods, such as Bel, the persecution of true believers, such as Stephen and Paul, and the warning against "false Christs and false prophets" (Mt 24:24):

> Then would they needs know, whether the bread in the box were God or no. I said, God is a Spirit, and will be worshipped in spirit and truth. Then they demanded, Will you plainly deny Christ to be in the sacrament? I answered, that I believe faithfully the eternal Son of God not to dwell there; in witness whereof I recited again the history of Bel. Dan. xiv; Acts vii–xvii; and Matt. xxiv, concluding thus: I neither wish death, nor yet fear his might; God have the praise thereof with thanks. (38–39)

The torments endured by Stephen and Paul are particularly
heartening for Askew's stand that "God was not in temples made
with hands" (6; cf. Acts 7:48, 17:25). In fact, biblical precedent
constantly inspires Askew's responses, whether in her decision "not
[to] throw pearls amongst swine, for acorns were good enough" (6;
cf. Mt 7:6), "not [to] sing a new song of the Lord in a strange land"
(30; cf. Ps 136/137:4) and, "being a woman," to abide—tauntingly—
by the Pauline directive not to "interpret the Scriptures, especially
where so many wise and learned men were" (21; cf. 1 Tim 2:11–12;
1 Cor 14:34). Her indebtedness to Paul focuses on an aspect different from the soteriology so evident in Julian of Norwich. Askew,
quite appropriately, stresses a faith alive to the sounds of battle and
equipped for its challenges. An identified citation—"If the trumpet
giveth an uncertain sound, who will prepare himself for the battle?"
(16; 1 Cor 14:8)—establishes her sense of alienation and discontent,
while the ballad she composed in Newgate, as the following stanzas
declare, illustrates this martyr's confidence in the protection of the
"whole armour of God" (Eph 6:13):

> Lyke as the armed knight
> Appointed to the feeld,
> With this world wyll I fight
> And fayth shalbe my shielde.
> Fayth is that weapon strong
> Which wyl not fayle at nede,
> My foes therfore amonge
> Ther with wil I procede.
> . . .
> Fayth in the fathers olde
> Obtayned rightewisenesse,
> Which make me very bolde
> To feare no worldes destresse.
> . . .
> Thou saiest lord, who so knocke
> To them wilt thou attende
> Undo therfore the locke
> And thy strong power sende. . . .

The account of her death is a testimony to this power. While the
officials set up a railed enclosure around St. Bartholomew's Church
in an attempt to control the crowds, Askew herself appears to have
gained renewed strength and conviction as an heroic interpreter:

The day of her execution being fixed, she was brought unto the stake at Smithfield in a chair, being unable to walk on account of her legs being dislocated by the rack. She was tied by the middle with a chain to the stake which held up her body. Dr. Shaxton, who once had embraced Christianity, but again fell back into papal idolatry, preached a sermon. When he spoke the truth Anne Askew assented to it, but when he spoke amiss, she exclaimed, There he misseth, and speaketh without book. . . . Then the lord Chancellor sent to Anne Askew letters, offering her the king's pardon if she would recant: she, refusing once to look upon them, made this answer again, that she came not thither to deny her Lord and Master.

Then the lord mayor ordered the fire to be put; and thus died this heroic, worthy, good woman. (51–52)

Jane Lead

Although more than a century separates the work of Jane Lead from the previous material, her writing is clearly part of this emergent Protestant tradition. Little known and not readily available, her books include a three-volume spiritual diary stretching over thirty years, *A Fountain of Gardens,* as well as at least fourteen other visionary works, detailing ecstasies, attesting to the presence of the "*Live Coal*" (*The Tree of Faith,* 61) in her hand, and fathoming the "Abyssal Deep" (*A Fountain of Gardens,* III, 249) to offer Wisdom's children "divine and spiritual Education" (*The Enochian Walks,* 28). Lead was the first major English proponent of the principles of the Silesian mystic Jacob Boehme, whom she studied in John Pordage's translation; but the distinctive features of her oracular, epiphanic style, scriptural borrowings, and preference for geometrical constructs stamp the writing of this visionary as more than mere regurgitation of the master.

Uncovering information about Lead is not easy. Errors in fact in certain conventionally reliable sources cloud the little that is knowable about her life, while critical bias in favor of orderly exposition complicates the issue of just assessment. The author of the *DNB* entry, Miss Fell Smith, for instance, refers to her short marriage and only child, when Mrs. Lead actually bore four daughters to her husband of twenty-seven years, upon whose death in 1670 she recorded in her diary that "then I resolved to make the choice of Anna, to wait in the Temple of the Lord day and night; and to be a

Widow indeed, after I had been the Wife of a Pious Husband about five and twenty years" (*A Fountain of Gardens*, II, "Epistle of the Author"); with damning succinctness Miss Fell Smith summarizes the prolific output of this widow in her sixties and seventies: "Her language is ungrammatical, her style involved, and her imagery fanciful and strained." Although, according to her son-in-law and devoted amanuensis, the Oxford Orientalist Dr. Francis Lee, "she always refused the title of prophetess when applied to her, saying that it was a burden to be called by such a title, and that she was not pleased with it" (Thune 215), Lead has been criticized on the very basis of her prophetic writings; for Howard Brinton they "obscure rather than reveal" (67) Behmenistic teaching, for Anne Judith Penny they owe unacknowledged debts to sixteenth century French and German authors (40), and, more recently, for Paul Korshin they afford evidence of "a slight touch of mental instability" (244) especially to a critic for whom Lead's pertinacity in remaining "in the queue for the Millennium" (245) appears a regrettable weakness. The only study in which Lead figures at all prominently, Nils Thune's *The Behmenists and the Philadelphians*, is now over forty years old; he evaluates her work "from a psychological point of view," noting that "her split and labile psyche found rest and inner harmony for a while in ecstasy," but is relieved to add that Lead "found a way back from her world of vivid dreams and hallucinations to a life of creative activity" (202). Desirée Hirst's examination of traditional symbolism, *Hidden Riches*, treats her more superficially and hurriedly, with the unsubstantiated observation that "Jane Lead was very conscious of her role as a woman, who, because of her sex, had special qualities as a spiritual leader" (171). Catherine Smith's essay in *Shakespeare's Sisters* is most interested in rehearsing Lead's voice for its antiphonal connections to Emily Dickinson, Adrienne Rich, and Sylvia Plath; Smith prizes as a central theme "one representative woman's awakening" (13) in the recovery of self-sufficiency through the discovery of Sophia.

As amazing as the slight treatment Lead has received from pre-feminist critics is her almost total neglect in feminist scholarship devoted to gnosticism, exegesis, and sapiential theology. Both Elaine Pagels and Pheme Perkins examine early gnostic texts with their reverence of female divine manifestations to prove either how liberal (for Pagels) or misogynous (for Perkins) these communities were; each reflects on the value of recuperating such texts today, but neither mentions Lead. Joan Engelsman exposes the systematic repression of the Sophia/Wisdom figure by the patriarchal clergy of the third and fourth centuries, but spends no time on the reemergence of Sophia in the works of this seventeenth century mystic. Virginia Mollenkott mines the Authorized Version for depictions of Yahweh's female ministrations and mentions Boehme, but Lead's highly idiosyncratic appropriation of biblical figures and roles goes unnoticed. In her study of the sapiential theology of Hildegard of Bingen, Barbara Newman announces her next project, a history of the Wisdom tradition, which will include Lead; but no doubt Newman's labeling of the "characteristic strain of . . . Hildegard's 'theology of the feminine' " as seeing "the feminine as a species of incapacity and frailty, yet also as a numinous and salvific dimension of the divine nature" (35–36) would have to be altered to suit Jane Lead who, despite failing eyesight, never described herself or other female figures as types of frailty.

Lead's frequent allusions to the Virgin Sophia and the androgynous Adam underscore her Behmenist tutelage. In Boehme's symbology, showing the influence of a variety of gnostic texts, God is "a dark compulsion to self-revelation" which unfolds, realizes, and fulfills its being in the process of reality; the mystic striving for inner worldly perfection sees in this process a form of self-salvation which "guarantees the establishment of a final man-made paradise within time" (Walsh 14–15). Wisdom permits forecasts of this state inasmuch as she reflects and contains the triune deity, which Boehme expands to a four-step entity: the ungrounded will of the Father, the comprehended will of the Son, and the outgoing Spirit all find themselves, as he expresses it in the *Mysterium Magnum*, in the eternal nothing of Wisdom.

> [Wisdom is] the eternal origin of all powers, colors and virtues, through which the threefold Spirit becomes desiring in this lust, namely for the powers, colors and virtues, and its desiring is an impressing, a comprehending of itself. (I: 6)

The Virgin Sophia does not give birth; rather, she reflects and sees. Calling to mind the depiction in Wisdom 7, Boehme argues in *Von der Menschwerdung Jesu Christi* (On the Incarnation of Jesus Christ)

> She is the dwelling place of the Spirit of God. . . . She is a mirror of the divinity, for each mirror is silent, and bears

no likeness except the likeness it receives. Thus the Virgin Wisdom is a mirror of divinity in which the Spirit of God beholds itself . . . and in Her the Spirit of God saw all the forms of creatures. . . . At the same time she is like the eye that sees. (I, 1:12)

Boehme's inclusion of Christ and Sophia in a single figure skews the central Christian tenet of the sacrificial atonement, just as his image of virginal Adam as part of this divinity makes the mystic's pursuit of the essence of Wisdom an attempt to recover an original human unity:

Christ and the virgin Sophia are only one person as the true human virgin of God, which Adam was before Eve when he was both man and woman and yet neither, but a virgin of God. (*Mysterium Magnum*, L:48)

For readers who now have access to the Nag Hammadi texts Boehme's androgynous Adam is an instance of the prevalence of an idea at least as old as the Gnostic Gospel of Philip, which makes the repeated claim that "when Eve was still in Adam death did not exist" (*Gospel of Philip* 68). In tracing some of the uses of the image of the androgyne in early Christianity, Wayne Meeks argues that Paul's original "baptismal reunification formula [Gal 3:28] . . . presupposes an interpretation of the creation story in which the divine image after which Adam was modeled was masculofeminine (185)," a "very common" myth according to Meeks in antiquity.

The links between Sophia and Adam and the stress on the indwelling, potentially transformative spirit provide the strongest evidence of Lead's Behmenistic discipleship. Yet despite her allusions to the potency of the "Deified Seed" within the "Paradisical Male and Female" and her vision of the self-sufficient reunion of the male, with "his Virgin in himself," and the female, with "her Male Power," rather than their union with one another, Lead's emphasis lies not in the Behmenistic ideals of self-salvation and man-made paradise. She concedes and refers throughout her work to the complex, awful, transcendent majesty of the divine, whose power is often revealed through Wisdom, corroborated by biblical passages, and manifest in a variety of symbolic constructs. In *The Heavenly Cloud Now Breaking: The Lord Christ's Ascension Ladder*, the knowledge of the resurrection, "proved by Scripture and Experience" (27), restores her flagging spirits to such an extent that she envisions God "as a flaming Wall, driving back that floating sea of Sensibility, and invading Spirits, shutting and binding them out of his own risen Body" (26). More frequently Lead describes this divine power in images which suggest a compelling internal superiority. In *The Wonders of God's Creation,* she rhapsodizes about "Inkindlings from his own immense Deep, which run as a Fiery Stream through me, so that I find there is no resisting this all-driving Power; by which hidden and unknown Worlds must be made manifest in this last Age of Times" (7–8). Within a few pages Lead is referring to the Virgin Wisdom's "secret deep," whose "Eternal Originality" she locates in "God the Tri-Un Deity, being a Virgin hid in Him from all Eternity" (31). Wisdom's animating powers, figured as "her Stone within you," cause her children to be "touched and changed . . . joyned to all these Flaming Stones" (79). With truly prophetic zeal Lead perorates about "this great and mighty Transmutation":

> Wherefore it is given me to advise you, that you give way to this Live Coal within you, that so it may burn away all the Dross and Tin, so as nothing but the Golden Matter, for Coagulation with the Deity may remain upon this Almighty and most sublime Thing, that is concealed in your inward Furnace. (79–80)

In the face of her overwhelmingly millenarian urge "to Proclaim another Day of Pentecost" (85), which, Korshin rightly observes, has inevitable analogues in contemporary politics and secular history, Lead's alchemical imagery of alembics and distillates only lasts until an apocalyptic warning about time running out takes is place:

> Take care, *O England,* lest this Star do from thee glide away: let not the Clouds of ignorant Suspicion or demurring Jealousie, concerning the true Heir of the New Jerusalem Mother, who is now to enter upon this Reign, and to rule with the Scepter of Faith, hinder thee from discovering that the Glass is now turn'd up, that its Half Hour is running, that the third watch is set, and that the Golden Cock is thereupon clapping his Wings. (*The Tree of Faith,* 221)

Just as the purposiveness of Lead's instruction and calls for awakening dispel a lot of the gloom of Boehme's dark compulsion in the Godhead, her deliberate invocation of spiritual authority and referents anchors her work within a Christian tradition which Boehme, who was labeled a heretic in his day, consciously leaves behind. Appropriately, Lead's chief interest in holy scripture is not to invoke a monolithic response but to examine its "Variety of Worlds" (*The Wonders of God's Creation*, 8). As Boehme's work partakes of the long-standing but often hidden gnostic tradition, so, too, Lead's theosophic exegesis about the coming of the third age of the Spirit recalls the considerably earlier work of the Cistercian reformer Joachim of Flora (d. 1208), whose *Concordantia Novi et Veteris Testamenti* (Harmony of the Old and New Testament) forecasts an age of the Holy Spirit when "spiritual men will have perfect spiritual understanding of the Scripture" (Smalley 288). A distant cousin of Joachim's, in some senses, Lead feels called to open "new Volumes" of the divine mind, which are to be available to the illumined rather than reserved for those in orders.

> The Old Testament having been appropriated to the Ministration of the Father, the New to the Son; now the Third Day is come, in which the Holy Ghost will have His, which will Excel all before it, to Unseal and Reveal what yet never was known or understood, that will be communicated to, and by such as are in an extraordinary manner sanctified and set apart for this holy Function. (8–9)

Thus designated and inspired, she writes prose and verse descriptions of her states of illumined, Wisdom-filled consciousness, which extend and at times reverse the meaning of biblical forms and figures. Korshin dismisses her verse as "atrocious" (244) and Smith queries the authenticity of her later poems produced under what she takes to be the repressive and patriarchal influence of Francis Lee. But, in an early mystical psalm—however much it might strain meter and switch metaphors—she pictures "Virgin-Wisdom's . . . Ship laden within" together with "the Lamb's pure Virgin-Bird" as types of Love; as I see it, the emphasis on tremendous internal activity, resulting in praise for the Almighty and dismissal of the world, nicely exemplifies the "metaphysical rebellion," "cosmic audacity" and "transcendent self-consciousness of the gnostic" (Meeks 207):

> We feel Love like a bubbling Spring,
> Which makes us the new Song ever sing.

All praises we will give to ELOHIM,
Who rideth on the SERAPHIMS:
Floods of Joy, with Coelestial Praise,
Shall now out-flow to the Ancient of Dayes;
For while we feel and taste Love's Fire,
It doth extinguish all earthly Desire.
(*The Revelation of Revelations*, 98)

Her use of biblical imagery is often precise and direct. In her preface to *A Fountain of Gardens* explaining the reasons for tying up her "bundle of Revelations" of the past thirty years, Lead borrows from the Song of Songs (4:12) to justify her preference in keeping this "Garden Enclosed," this "Fountain Sealed." When she recounts her first visitation from "God's Eternal Virgin-Wisdom," however, Lead's scriptural appropriations involve sex and role changes. Wisdom offers to become Rebecca to Lead's Jacob:

> . . . a true natural mother; for out of my Womb thou shalt
> be brought forth after the manner of a Spirit, Conceived
> and Born again: this thou shalt know by a New Motion of
> Life, stirring and giving a restlessness, till Wisdom be
> born again within the inward parts of thy soul. (I, 18)

When she advises about loyalty soon afterward, Wisdom assumes the role of the Nazirite, instructing Lead in the way to become "his Dalilah . . . of perfect beauty and spotless Chastity."

> Then his Head on thy Lap he will repose, and his hidden
> strength to thee reveal, and nothing from thee conceal,
> being in Joint-Union, no more twain, but one Spirit: The
> seven locks of his Power he will suffer thee to unloose . . .
> as may slay and overcome the Philistines Host, which such
> prickling Bryars have been to invade thy inward Coasts
> and most holy Place. (I, 43)

Although Lead adds no marginal biblical citations, her borrowings are nevertheless easy to trace. The travel and assumption of the antediluvian patriarch (Gen 5:24) supply the context of her "Experimental Account" of Mount-Sion visions in *The Enochian Walks with God,* a book which closes with Lead's depiction of the restorative effects of the divine word as akin to Elijah's healing of the widow's son (1 Kgs 17:21–22); comparing "these Communications . . . to Elijah's stretching himself upon the dead child," Lead admits: "I found a precious feeding hereupon, and did feel such a spreading and quickning Life come upon me, as if all were filled with Christ in every part" (34).

Geometric shapes, such as circles and triangles, often serve to clarify visions or reify doctrines in a way that is reminiscent of the pillars, temples, figures, and liturgical objects of Hildegard of Bingen's *Scivias* and *De Operatione Dei*. These constructs are, admittedly, more developed and expansive in Hildegard; moreover, I am not suggesting any direct influence of the eleventh century, encyclopedically accomplished, and renowned Rhenish sibyl on the seventeenth century visionary living in obscurity in London. The differences between these two mystics are actually more instructive than the likenesses. As the abbess of a Benedictine convent, Hildegard showed an unsurprising preference for images invoking the hierarchy and the magisterium, in representations of Ecclesia, apostles, prophets, martyrs, nuns, and monks; as a devout layperson who championed a Protestant mystic, Jane Lead favored more pluralist constructs, with less demarcations of rank and sex. In the "visional appearance" recorded for 15 July 1694, for instance, she describes four concentric circles, radiating from the "Pure white Glass of Light" surrounding "the Personal Prince of Glory" and victorious, faithful "Elders," to the "Azure Blue-Circle" of those "numerous Persons . . . waiting . . . to break through into Mount-Sion-Principle," to the "Pale-Lightning" of the third circle comprised of Seraphims and Cherubims ministering to those in the second and fourth, to the "Dusky-Colour" of the fourth consisting of "those who were yet to be gathered in and born again" (*The Enochian Walks with God*, 37). A similarly inclusive and encouraging logic, blending initiates and outsiders, lies behind her vision of the heart of the deity as a series of encased and interlocking triangles (Figure 2). Her explication of the central interlocking triangles showcases Wisdom at the same time as it challenges the invited multitude to eschew mere worldliness:

> From this Idea, I had great and full Confirmation that the Heart of the Trinity was most free, and ready to embrace and receive them, who of one Spirit and Heart were together fixed, to break through the Golden Chain, so as none might be nearer to the Heart of the Trinity than such who have rent and divided from all Creaturely Hearts, that so they might know what from this Triangle-

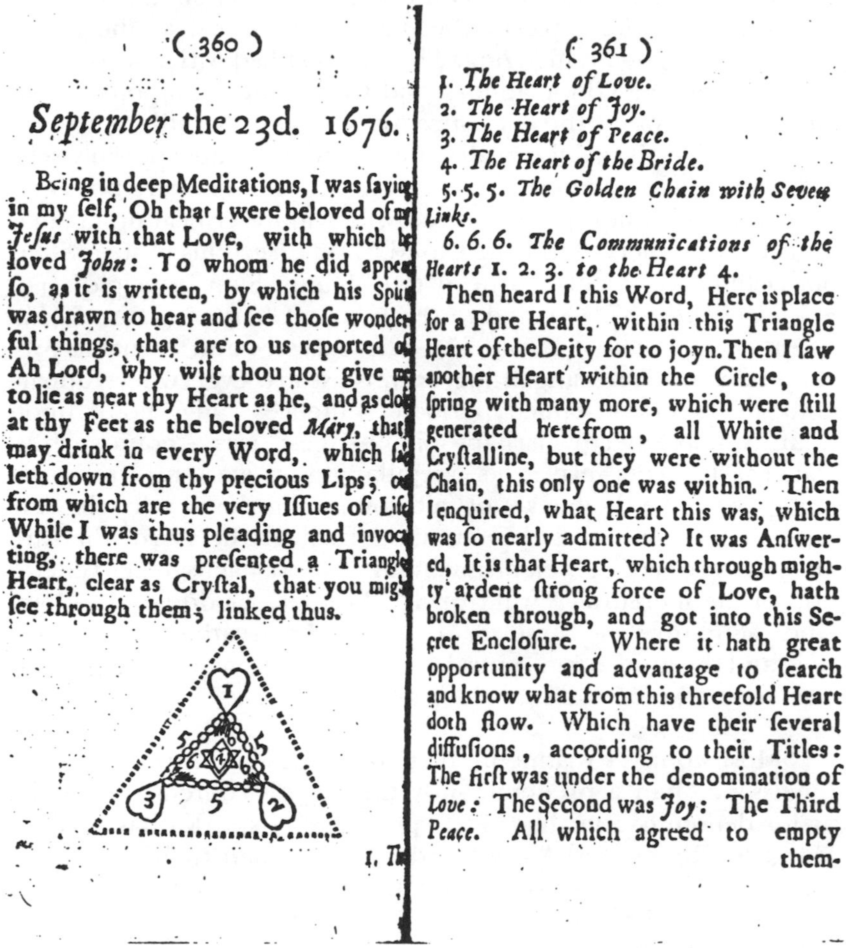

(360)

September the 23d. 1676.

Being in deep Meditations, I was saying in my self, Oh that I were beloved of *Jesus* with that Love, with which he loved *John*: To whom he did appear so, as it is written, by which his Spirit was drawn to hear and see those wonderful things, that are to us reported of. Ah Lord, why wilt thou not give me to lie as near thy Heart as he, and as close at thy Feet as the beloved *Mary*, that may drink in every Word, which falleth down from thy precious Lips; or from which are the very Issues of Life. While I was thus pleading and invocating, there was presented a Triangle Heart, clear as Crystal, that you might see through them; linked thus.

(361)

1. The Heart of Love.
2. The Heart of Joy.
3. The Heart of Peace.
4. The Heart of the Bride.
5. 5. 5. The Golden Chain with Seven Links.
6. 6. 6. The Communications of the Hearts 1. 2. 3. to the Heart 4.

Then heard I this Word, Here is place for a Pure Heart, within this Triangle Heart of the Deity for to joyn. Then I saw another Heart within the Circle, to spring with many more, which were still generated herefrom, all White and Crystalline, but they were without the Chain, this only one was within. Then I enquired, what Heart this was, which was so nearly admitted? It was Answered, It is that Heart, which through mighty ardent strong force of Love, hath broken through, and got into this Secret Enclosure. Where it hath great opportunity and advantage to search and know what from this threefold Heart doth flow. Which have their several diffusions, according to their Titles: The first was under the denomination of *Love*: The Second was *Joy*: The Third *Peace*. All which agreed to empty them-

Figure 2.
From Jane Lead's *A Fountain of Gardens*, Vol. 1

Heart of *Love, Joy,* and *Peace,* doth ever flow. (*A Fountain of Gardens,* I, 362)

Jane Lead's poetic prose and symbolic narrative can have a peculiar effect on twentieth century readers. Their hold can be magnetic, and the force of the diction—as much as the act of understanding—mesmerizing. They are so filled with end-rhymed sentences, extended metaphors, and hyphenated compounds that I began to think of the enclosure, the cocoon, the little sanctuary they afforded. But I also realized how awkward and possibly self-indulgent such reactions would seem to those who were not Lead fans, who were not quite as rapt by, but more critical of, emanations from a "Fiery-Baptizing Cloud," and directions to strip "This Sin-Defiling-Garment," to heed the "Mount-Sion-Principle" (*The Enochian Walks,* 37–38), and to reach "to a Christed Stature" (*The Ascent to the Mount of Vision,* 35). The excesses and arguable presumptions of the evangelizing enthusiast are everywhere apparent: she favors sustained periodic sentences; piles noun upon noun to make her own rhapsodic linkages; uses a noun such as "tabernacle" as a verb in its irregular figurative sense; relies on metaphors, like the bucket of faith plumbing the depths, the furnace of the soul, and the munition rock of the Lord, that are amazingly concrete, even prosaic, and never slackens in her veneration of the mercurial Virgin-Bride, -Mother, -Goddess, -Wisdom. And yet, in my view, these very excesses, the breathlessly honorific style and the animating, central, potentiating female figure of Wisdom define Jane Lead's theology of the feminine.

Most women's writing in the middle ages and throughout the renaissance had a predominantly theological content. While the major denominations had their spokespersons in Katharine Parr, Margaret Roper, and Mary Ward, the sects had their propagandists too, with Anna Trapnel for the Baptists, Elizabeth Hooten and Margaret Fell for the Quakers, and Elizabeth Warren for the old-style Puritans. Both Roper, Thomas More's daughter, and Parr, Henry VIII's sixth wife, were accomplished scholars, at ease in discussing theology. Not every female spoke with impunity, however. Mary Ward's active, unenclosed congregation of women, the Institute of the Blessed Virgin Mary, was suppressed in 1631 because of its members' so-called lack of maidenly reserve. Hooten, the first woman Quaker minister, suffered repeated imprisonments in England and America, and Trapnel's rhapsodic versified prophesying, especially its criticism of Cromwell, sent her to Bridewell. Their interpretive work, following in the tradition of so many Continental forerunners, showed what a multi-purpose volume the Bible remained. Because such writing as Margaret Fell's *Women's speaking justified, proved and allowed of by the Scriptures* (1666), Joanna Southcott's *The Strange Effects of Faith* (1801) and *A Dispute Between the Woman and the Powers of Darkness* (1802), and Anna Wheeler's *Appeal of One-Half the Human Race* (1825) used biblical sources to stress themes of enslavement, pain, and privation, their images of female defiance relate them more to contemporary feminist exegesis than to medieval devotional literature. Despite the fact that the reactions of visionaries and reformers, ascetics and activists to the Bible have been so diverse, the common feature uniting them is equally remarkable. As practical observers of the world around them, they all made scripture the lens through which to assess and the text on which to found their social commentaries.

It was not long before a focus on a specific readership controlled the efforts of some very purposive and pragmatic interpreters. The women who apprehended biblical topics as a way of instructing children, as distinct from those who described visions and ecstasies or produced tracts and diatribes, merit special consideration, which will be the subject of the next chapter.

4
Governesses and Matriarchs:
Milk for Babes

In *Adam's* fall
We sinned all.
This *Book* attend,
Thy life to mend.
The *Cat* does play
And after slay.
—*The Child's Guide*

As soon, therefore, as a child can read fluently, and is capable of having any part of the Scriptures explained to him, in a *practical way, that part* should be put into his hands, and *other parts in succession,* till he has obtained such a general knowledge of the contents of the Bible, as may enable him to read any portion of Scripture with pleasure and edification.
—Mrs. Trimmer, *Essay on Christian Education,*
Section XIII

Persons and occurrences noted in the Scripture do not, like stars, all show brightness; far from it: over many of them is spread the dismal darkness of our fallen nature. But it is by looking upon the fallen nature that we are prepared to admire the blessed contrast. The dismal darkness is our own; for we all partake of the same fallen nature: but the starlike brightness is the reflected shining of divine grace and mercy.
—Mrs. Dalby, *Dutch Tiles*

The Duty To Instruct

Contemporary readers' responses to early works of children's literature can vary sharply. They may be charmed by the line drawings of the fair, pajama-clad English orphan, Little Henry, clinging to the shoulders of his adult Hindu friend, Boosy; they can also be appalled by Mrs. Sherwood's transparent moralizing ploys in *Little Henry and His Bearer* (1814), which make the cherubic seven year old into a sentimental scripture-quoting catechist and reduce his Indian servant to a status-less convert. Similarly, readers of mid-Victorian picture books, such as Miss Corner's *Scriptural Tales* (1857), *Routledge's Scripture Gift-Book* (1866), and *Sunday Afternoons with Mamma* (1866), might be attracted by the vivid hand-colored illustrations or Kronheim plates, but perplexed by the messages of docility and absolute obedience which the accompanying texts routinely convey.

Discussing these "godly" works in a late twentieth century context, then, really requires several adjustments. First of all, our sense that we are a multiplicity of selves, that we are always changing and becoming, and that we have grown through infancy and childhood to be relatively autonomous agents hardly jibes with this literature's repeated directives to listen, obey, and submit. Besides, we find its hortatory seriousness difficult to relate to the more modern theories of child development, from Piaget and Bruner to Freud and Jung. Generally speaking, readers no longer recognize either the prominence of Lydia, Damaris, Priscilla, and Eunice as catechetical models or the urgent and unequivocal nature of parental moral teaching. The unrelieved rigor and war against so-called laxity in these works might prompt today's readers to wonder about possible hysterical disorders or overdeveloped superegos.

A histrionic example, from Maria Edgeworth's play *Dumb Andy*, in which the child himself cries out for direction, may clarify the differences between then and now, and let us see how rooted in the conditions and imperatives of the adult world children's literature has always been. *Dumb Andy* is one of Edgeworth's three *Little Plays for Young People; Warranted Harmless* (1827); its crisis brings the issue of parental duty in moral instruction to a head. In the climactic scene the boy-hero, an orphan raised by gypsies and taught to play dumb to bring in money, experiences such a moral dilemma that he "throws the hat from his head, falls down on his knees, [and] bursts into tears." When he can no longer deceive the good family who is befriending him, "Dumb" Andy's conflict be-

Frontispiece of a Victorian edition (1886) of Favell Lee Bevan's
*The Peep of Day; or, A Series of the Earliest Religious Instruction the
Infant Mind is Capable of Receiving.*

tween inherent honor and sense of gratitude takes the form of this outburst:

> I do not deserve it! I am not deaf! I am not dumb! I am a cheat!—But oh! I don't know whether I am doing wrong or right, now this minute. (*looking up to Heaven*)—Oh! if I knew which was right to do!—But I have no mother, no father—*none* to teach me. Oh! if I'm wrong, now, I can't help it—I could not stand your goodness and your pity of me (*sobbing*). I could not!—I could not!—that's the trial I could not stand—anything but that! and I would never have spoken. They might have flogged me as long as they could stand over me. (*starting up and changing his look and tone*)—Oh! I promised I would not tell—I promised!— and I've broke my word—and this is worse—Oh! worse than all I done! (148–150)

Although modern listeners may be shocked or even incensed by the fever pitch of the child's punitive awareness of wrongdoing, the audience of Maria Edgeworth, an esteemed and more or less secular behaviorist of her day, likely applauded this poignant exposition of the duty to instruct.

Difficult to accept though it may be for readers whose knowledge or memories of children's literature start around the 1950s, the idea that everyday incidents and objects could conceivably motivate lessons about eternal life was, from the outset, a cardinal tenet in literature designed to prepare children for the fulfillment of "man's chief end": in the words of the *Shorter Catechism*, "to glorify God and enjoy Him forever." The trusting child who responded to the challenge of creating heaven on earth was a prime example of the duality that informs all catechetical and moral literature. In keeping with the Marcan pericope (10:13), he was the model recipient of the kingdom, "the Christian's example," as John Earle's *Microcosmographie* (1633) characterized him: "Could hee put off his body with his little Coate, he had got eternitie without a burthen, and exchang'd but one Heaven for another" (2). Henry Vaughan's desire to retreat to the "white Celestiall thought" of his "Angell-infancy" ("The Retreate," lines 6, 2) and Robert Herrick's vision— and amazing assessment in the comparative degree—of "that whiter island, where / Things are evermore sincere" ("The White Island," lines 9–10) draw attention to the dominant color surrounding the child as incarnation of goodness. But, as innumerable warnings attest, he was also the diminutive sinner, daubed with "sulling coal or pitch," in John Bunyan's words, and manifestly "unfitted/ To be to heaven admitted" (*A Book for Boys and Girls,* 61, 6). Hence, Thomas White's *A Little Book for Little Children* (1660) exhorted the reader to be "as little a childe as can be," assuring him that for heavenly entrance "the lesser the better, the more welcome" (13); yet James Talbott's *The Christian School-Master* (1707) enjoined teachers and parents to be careful of the impressionable "Minds of Children, like blank Paper or smooth Wax," and to set about inculcating the crucial lesson: "the Chief Concern of our Life, to know what is of the greatest Importance to our Happiness in this and the next World" (17).

Belief in the influences and consequences of child-rearing was not confined to any specific sect or denomination. As a matter of fact, it is remarkable to note—and especially throughout the political and religious fractiousness of sixteenth to nineteenth century England—how widespread this belief actually was and also how, allowing for certain catechetical colorations or emphases, it served to unite Recusants, Puritans, Methodists, Dissenters, and Church of England Evangelicals. Mary Jackson has summarized the central and unifying principle succinctly: "the belief that individuals must be able to read for themselves the documents of salvation made Bible reading among even the lowliest acceptable" (30).

The Need To Be Literate

As inheritors and advocates of this moral tradition, the women who composed abecedaria, catechisms, hymns, verse, allegories, dramas, and stories for the young did so in the fervent conviction that such introductions to literacy also laid the foundations for upright living and eternal happiness. That sweeping statement, along with its underlying assumption, requires a lot of qualification. The sense of righteousness in much of this religious writing is undeniable. So too are the deliberate differences in tone, vocabulary, and intention when these women address poor restive youngsters and cossetted middle-class ones; the former were to show industry and stay in their place, while the latter were to learn charity (certainly not to be confused with socialism), patience, and responsibility. It is a bit of a simplification to say that the standard was obedience; it was probably closer to tractability.

Consider, for instance, the rudimentary stereotyping and direct commands of Sarah Trimmer's *The Charity School Spelling Book*

(1785), with stories of "good and bad boys" and "good and bad girls" in two separate parts. Mrs. Trimmer's views of the usefulness and thrift of the poor are entirely undisguised:

> The Girl spins fine yarn.
> The Boy heads pins well.
> The Boy mends his own coat.
> The Girl makes the boy's shirt.
> Good Girls make their own clothes.
> Good Boys take care of their shoes. (16)

Immediately following the alphabet Trimmer inserts these injunctions, showing the necessary link between literacy and docility:

> If you would be wise and good, you must learn to read your Book. No one likes rude Boys and Girls, they get beat and chid. Those who are rich will not help those who are poor, if they will not try to be good. (17–18)

Whether on a daily or weekly basis, schooling in Trimmer's estimate is inextricably connected to religion. Convinced that "religious education is an EVERY DAY BUSINESS" and that "parents of the lower orders are not capable of instructing their children," she nevertheless stopped short of endorsing the Lancastrian system of large group instruction (700–800 pupils at a time) because of its "neglect of catechizing" (*A Comparative View*, 10, 125). By citing and alluding to the Bible as often and insistently as she does, Mrs. Trimmer established herself, in a manner continued by the Reverend Legh Richmond's *Annals of the Poor* a generation later, as an "authorized administrator and interpreter" (Kelly 181) of this text of texts.

Although the emphasis of A.L.O.E. (A Lady of England: Charlotte Tucker), in her extended pedagogical allegory *The Crown of Success* (1863), is every bit as pragmatic as Trimmer's, she delineates the social threat of illiteracy against a comfortable mercantile backdrop of shops and prices. The first obstacle the protected but illiterate Desley children encounter in their approach to the town of Education and especially at the shop of Messrs. Reading and Writing is the proprietary dwarf-porter, Mr. Alphabet, who "was just twenty-six inches high, and had a head almost as big as the rest of his body" (32). Before entering Mr. Reading's "fine shop," each child must pay a toll of bright hours; the slowest and fattest, Lubin, is forced to pay double and even subjected to ridicule by his quick older brother, who prates " 'If you can't master little ABC, a precious poor creature you must be' " (34).

Attitudes were, of course, inculcated at the same time as literacy was being learned. A late eighteenth century chapbook copy of the anonymous "Factory Child's Hymn" encourages a different form of acceptance from that promoted by Mary Ann Kilner's unperturbed heroine in *Jemima Placid* (1783). When, due to his wife's illness, the Reverend Placid, vicar of Smiledale, must send his daughter to live with his sister in London, the "amiable," "always-contented," "good humored" and "agreeable" Jemima is a real curiosity to her ill-tempered, fretful, and undisciplined cousins. In conversation after conversation the unchanging paragon, a forerunner of Pollyanna, extols the advantages of docility. At one point she goes as far as versifying a consolation for her cousin, whose planned outing has been canceled because of a rainfall:

> Then Eleanor tell me, what joy should I find,
> In the discord of passion, the storm of the mind?
> Tho' the elements will not resign to my sway,
> My own temper, I trust, reason's voice will obey;
> I can make to my fate my desires resign,
> And the joys of contentment will ever be mine. (102)

Though equally saccharine, the working child's lesson, a more explicit preachment about reward deferred, also involves greater sweat and risk:

> When to my work, through cold and sleet,
> I haste, with feet all bare,
> I think upon the Golden Street
> And smiling sunshine there
>
> And when the noise is loud and long
> Of engines ever near,
> I think, how beautiful the song
> Which angel-children hear!
>
> And I am happy all the day,
> Whatever task is given,
> Because I know this is the way
> God trains my soul for heaven.

Changing Scholarly Perceptions

Critical commentary on this literature is, slowly, starting to incorporate historical and cultural studies. Ivy Pinchbeck and Margaret Hewitt have examined the development of parish workhouses, Schools of Industry, and Colleges of Infants as schemes organized to teach, in fact compel, non-vagrant children "to labour to support themselves and relieve the poor rates" (160). As to the prevailing bourgeois ideologies in writing for the young, Isaac Kramnick has sifted through eighteenth and nineteenth century examples to make a strong case that "children's literature has been designed to serve ideological objectives" (203), socializing young learners to middle class values. J.H. Plumb tidily sums up the importance of eighteenth century children, particularly lower middle class youngsters, as "counters in the parents' social aspirations" (80). Social immobility in "working class culture," by contrast, is the theme Thomas Laqueur sees reiterated in the imprints of the Sunday School Union, the Society for Promoting Religious Knowledge (SPCK), and the Religious Tract Society (RTS). As Lionel Adey's survey of nineteenth century hymnals clarifies, class-conditioning remained a constant feature; though he cites many examples which distorted the Christian ethic "into a spineless resignation" (91), his observation on a hymn common to a public school hymn book and a council school hymnal underlines the inculcation of concepts of social class: "Plebeian and patrician could each sing this entire text according to his expectations, whether of drudgery or of responsible office" (95).

Several studies focus directly on the ways in which prevailing and often secular adult assumptions shaped the direction and content of religious literature for the young. Samuel Pickering investigates the continuing influence of John Locke especially in Evangelical circles. Doreen Rosman debunks the stereotypes about Evangelicals as grim, Bible-quoting isolationists, and concentrates instead on their role as fond guardians in homes characterized by "the easiness of the relationship between parent and child" (104) and a "close father/child affection" (107). By discerning the systematic connections between literary developments and "the larger sociopolitical context," Mary Jackson provides an interpretive history of the development of juvenile literature, showing "how and why Puritan values eventually prevailed" (x,xi).

One of the most subscribed-to explanations of the progress and development of literature for children involves the gradual and successful secularizing of the material, its steady march away from Bible-based training and toward imaginative enrichment. For many theorists this march entails a repudiation of the past with all its strictness about sin and lessons about contentment and an honest embrace of human fallibility. A recent example of such argumentation is the adversarial manner of Geoffrey Summerfield's *Fantasy and Reason;* in his damnation of Puritans and Evangelicals, he stacks the cards unjustly against the "petty-minded" and "sadistic" (76) Dr. Watts, the "philistine," coarse-spirited (205) Mrs. Trimmer, and the "unsympathetic and uneven" (220) Mrs. Barbauld. As a movement away from the clammy morbidity of moralizing, this line of argument reminds me a good deal of David Copperfield's finding himself "more dead than alive" in the Blunderstone church and daydreaming about "what a good place [the pulpit] would be to play in, and what a castle it would make, with another boy coming up the stairs to attack it, and having the velvet cushions with the tassels thrown down on his head" (9). Although the young observer takes refuge in fantasies, Dickensian churches and pulpits are usually more solemn, ominous, and funereal. Paul Dombey's christening, preceded by a joyless wedding, is "a cold and dismal scene" indeed, set in a "chill and earthy" place, with a "tall shrouded pulpit" amidst "the dreary perspective of empty pews . . . empty benches . . . and cold stone slabs," and lit with a "cadaverous light" (35–36). In *Bleak House,* the little Lincolnshire church in the park onto which Lady Dedlock's windows open is so "mouldy" that "the oaken pulpit breaks out into a cold sweat" (6). More ammunition to support the repudiation of the past comes from the satirical revolts of Ernest Pontifex looking back on the "sickly, debilitating debauch" (8) of his upbringing in *The Way of All Flesh* and Edmund Gosse solemnly muttering in the face of his father's "dogmatic theology" (57) that "The Lord has not come, the Lord will never come," and thus crumbling "the artificial edifice of extravagant faith" (165).

A less extreme and possibly more accurate index, I submit, of the growth and breadth of children's literature is provided in the almost forgotten tale by Mrs. Gatty, "Imperfect Instruments." A clergyman's wife and mother of a large family in mid-Victorian England, friend of Tennyson and opponent of Darwin, amateur scientist (specializing in seaweed) and founder-editor of *Aunt Judy's Magazine* (with stories for children and reviews of books for them), Margaret Gatty might appear to be the quintessential type of the well-intentioned storyteller for the young. But although her parable from nature is about the quest for perfection, it is, in fact, an acknowledgement of imperfection. Moreover, although the catechisms and allegories, verses and hymns, essays and sermons, dramas and stories of the moral tradition are viewed customarily as dinning the lesson of the pursuit of perfection, they actually tend more and more, especially in the late eighteenth and throughout the nineteenth century, to be expositions of fallibility, with appropriate additives of remorse and gratitude for instruction. Like the clergyman's son, an eager curate, in "Imperfect Instruments," who, wanting to improve the sound of the church's organ, must learn, as the old organ-builder remarks, that his tuning was "too perfect by half" and that "the system's perfect, but if you stick too close to it, it sets you wrong" (81), the child characters in the most mature of moral literature for children are not absolute paragons. In Gatty's story father and son debate in biblical paraphrases— though they might remind us a little of Escalus and Angelo:

> "Measure me the measure of the right," cried the troubled father, "as compared with the impressions it will cause. You cannot drive straight lines through life without knocking over good feelings as well as bad ones."
> "The right way is a narrow way," replied the son; "to trim to the prejudices of the ignorant is to sacrifice principle to man-pleasing." (74)

Allusions to the Authorized Version inform their talk and serve as hinges in their story, which is nonetheless about "irregularity— inconsistency—contradictions . . . in the material world as in the spiritual" (82). In their avowedly moral works for children, the women writers, who in large measure maintained this tradition, interpreted the Bible for their audience as a means to literacy and principled living and, in some of the best examples, as a way of understanding human ironies and inconsistencies.

Catechisms

The least flexible of the instructional modes would appear to be the catechism with its expected parroting of "precept upon precept" (Is 28:10). One of the most prolific composers of infant and advanced catechisms, abridgements of the scriptures, collections of sacred history, prayer book companions, religious tracts, and edifying stories was Sarah Trimmer. She fashioned the continued *Essay on Christian Education* (1802–1805) into a veritable manifesto, declaring that "we would not have the BIBLE itself put out of sight" and appealing to elders as Christian pragmatists in the observation that "a child who is instructed through the medium of the Scripture will give much less trouble to parents than those who are kept in ignorance of the Bible" (Section XIV, II, 299). Trimmer remained the revered doyenne of the moral tradition throughout the nineteenth century. She no doubt influenced such works as Mrs. Sherwood's *Stories Explanatory of the Church Catechism* (1817), in which Mary, an insipid mouthpiece, enters mechanically and cravenly into one conversation after another with her godmother, and Favell Lee Bevan's *The Peep of Day* (1833) and *Line Upon Line* (1838), in which catechetical instruction is presented in the form of a basal reader and Bible stories are abbreviated and summarized, usually concluding with doggerel of Bevan's own devising. Mrs. Dalby's *Dutch Tiles* (1842) contrived the pretext of a conversation between mother and son on the topic of the ornamental tiles around the fireplace which happen, unsurprisingly, to depict biblical scenes; despite the setting's coziness, the ensuing talk is a series of leaden accounts of Bible history.

The gap separating the colloquial exchanges between Maria and her Mamma, in Dorothy Kilner's *First Principles of Religion, and the Existence of a Deity, explained in a series of dialogues adapted to the capacity of the infant mind* (c. 1787), from versified placebos and matriarchal directives might suggest a vastly different understanding of catechesis. Although the chatterbox Maria sounds willful and almost rude by contrast to more docile Georgian and Victorian counterparts, her curiosity about basic concepts, such as the origins of people and objects, and the nature of Godhead, prayer, and the Bible, sparks all of the dialogues and also accounts for the distinctive emphases of a religious primer organized around this premise:

> Nobody can think a child of three or seven years old should be argued with as a grown person. Long discourses, and philosophical reasonings, at best amaze and confound, but do not instruct children.

As an instructress Mamma, who is not a know-it-all, is often flummoxed by her child's queries, which have the effect of backing her into a corner.

Frontispiece of Dorothy Kilner's *First Principles of Religion*
(c. 1787).

Frontispiece of Lucy Barton's *Bible Letters for Children* (1831).

Maria. Who made the Bible?
Mamma. It has been made a vast number of years.
Maria. But who made it?
Mamma. Some very good men wrote it, that every body might know how to be good, and do what God pleased.
Maria. But how did these men know what God would please?
Mamma. Because God directed and taught them what to write, and therefore they were sure it was what God pleased.
Maria. How did God direct and teach them?
Mamma. I don't know.
Maria. Why don't you know?
Mamma. Because I do *not.* There are a great many things about God I cannot explain.
Maria. I thought you knew everything, Mamma.
Mamma. Then, my dear, you were very much mistaken, for there is a great number of things I know nothing of, nor cannot understand. (24)

Maria is a single-minded questioner, determined to extract a response that suits her; for instance, she demands a prompt and satisfying answer about "where God is":

Maria. Why can't you tell me *now?* I want to hear now, and I want to know where God is, that I may see God. (12)

The child's frustration, in trying to attach a gender to God, is not dispelled by her mother's stolid refusal to compare and speculate:

Maria. If God is not a man, is God a woman? or what is God?
Mamma. I never saw God: but I know that God is neither a man or a woman, or like any thing in the world. But I know that God is very kind and good, and loves all good people. (14)

The candor and resilience of Maria—in many ways a precursor of Edgeworth's Rosamond—make her an endearingly real child, who admits being distracted in church ("always thinking about something else, and looking about") and wanting to say long prayers with a very pragmatic aim ("to ask God to give me things, and to make God love me"). Maria is proud of her acts of charity, but shocked by

the "naughtiness" of poor boys, until her mother explains that their
"fathers and mothers are out all day working very hard, to get a little
money to buy them some victuals, and have no time to teach them"
(43). With her believable middle-class lapses and prejudices Maria is
still a more enjoyable character than the readily available paragons.
Mamma with her literal-minded, prosaic, and unquestioning trust
in biblical texts might seem to be evading the work of interpretation,
yet within the mode of a realistic conversation *First Principles* has
succeeded in addressing the fundamental catechetical questions of
who made the earth and man and to what end.

Hymns and Verse

Hymns and verse are another means of purposive, instructional discourse. In the late eighteenth century Evangelicalism con-
tributed to the spread of moral literature explicitly designed,
through characterizations and plot structure, to appeal to and pac-
ify the lower class.

Many of Hannah More's *Cheap Repository Tracts* (1795–ff),
printed to be sold in bulk to the gentry and middle classes and
distributed free to the laboring classes, were versified accounts of
the stabilizing influence of the word. More exorcized a lot of her
impatience with indolent, gin-swilling common folk in such lessons
by negative example as that of Sinful Sally, who from her prison cell
owns that her dereliction to her present pox-ridden state began at
the time she abandoned sacred and turned to profane reading:

> Now I lay my Bible by
> Chuse that impious book so new
> Love the bold blaspheming lie
> And that filthy novel too.

In keeping with her admitted purpose to show the tranquilizing
and restorative aspects of religion and social order, More does not
present a prosperous bawd (no Moll Flanders for the Cheap Repository Tracts!); after having sent several lovers to the gallows, a
dying Sal prays for assistance:

> Thou can'st save the vilest harlot,
> Grace I've heard is free and full,
> Sins that once were "red as scarlet,"
> Thou can'st make "as white as wool."

Although she displays a certain lurid fascination with crime and malefactors, More is definitely most at ease in dealing with sterling lessons by positive example, as in "Patient Joe; or, The Newcastle Collier" and "Dan and Jane; or, Faith and Works." With his controlling belief in Providence, fortified by daily Bible reading, Patient Joe is the type of the contented laborer; further, his story metes out the appropriate rough justice, in More's view, to idle unbelievers like Tim Jenkins, "who drank and who gam'd, / Who mock'd at his Bible, and was not asham'd." Jenkins is killed in a cave-in at the pit, while Joe, who had been chasing the dog that filched his dinner, returns to sermonize:

> Thus events great and small, if aright understood,
> Will be found to be working together for good.
> "When my meat," Joseph cry'd, "was just now stol'n awāy,
> And I had no prospect of eating today,
> How could it appear to a short-sighted sinner,
> That my life would be sav'd by the loss of my dinner."

The tracts' delineation of contentment is one of their most problematic features. The long-suffering, impecunious shepherd of Salisbury Plain, another daily Bible reader, is a troubling incarnation of the beatitudes, especially in his meek reliance on handouts from the gentry. The dynamic activity of More herself— among other things, setting up a charity school in Cheddar after she and her sisters were appalled to find in a parish of 2000 a single Bible and "that used to prop up a flower pot"[1]—stands in curious contrast to the passivity and quietism she promoted.

Though Anna Barbauld's ideas about the uneducated and delinquent were just as vociferous as More's, Barbauld did make special concessions to children in attempting to explain biblical mysteries and Christian eschatology. She even broke ranks with the uniformly admired Dr. Watts by writing her hymns in prose, not verse. As I read it, Barbauld's *Hymns in Prose* (1781) is also essentially different in tone from such contemporaneous works as Charles Wesley's *Hymns for Children* (1763) and Rowland Hill's *Divine Hymns Attempted in Easy Language for the Use of Children* (1790). Since most of Charles' hymns for children were included in the *Collection of Hymns, for the Use of the People Called Methodists* (1780), it seems safe to assume that he did not believe in any special status or attenuated sentiments for the young. John actually pointed to his brother's main differences from Watts as a writer for children, in not letting himself "down to them" but rather in lifting "them up to us." He explained the Wesleyan hymns as the obverse of Watts' songs:

> They contain strong and manly sense, yet expressed in such plain and easy language as even children may understand. But when they do understand them they will be children no longer, only in years and in stature. (VII: 132)

The opposite philosophy prevails with the popular preacher and first chairman of the Religious Tract Society, Rowland Hill. Having modeled his hymns "as an Appendix to Dr. Watts's *Divine Songs*," he recommended them especially for Sunday School children, although his Preface noted that they would be "not less acceptable to children of a superior description." Hill groups his readers in clearly defined chronological and socio-economic categories and proceeds to supply them with what he considers appropriately simplified fare. *Hymns in Prose* corresponds neither to Wesley's baroque tapestry of praise nor to Hill's depiction of children as sedate recipients of God's love.

Even though the text is replete with the archaisms of the Authorized Version, Barbauld's tone is conversational and engaging. As the last of the fifteen hymns testifies, she uses the deceptively simple cadences of the psalmist to comment on transient mortality and its apocalyptic equivalent. The opening stresses the vicissitudes of mere earthly beauty.

> The rose is sweet, but it is surrounded with thorns; the lily of the valley is fragrant, but it springeth up amongst the brambles. The spring is pleasant, but it is soon past: the summer is bright, but the winter destroyeth the beauty thereof.
>
> The rainbow is very glorious, but it soon vanisheth away: life is good, but it is quickly swallowed up in death. (98)

Barbauld transmutes many aspects of this temporal scene in sketching eternal beauty.

> There is a land where the roses are without thorns, where the flowers are not mixed with brambles.

In that land there is eternal spring, and light without any cloud.

The tree of life groweth in the midst thereof; rivers of pleasures are there, and flowers that never fade.

Myriads of happy spirits are there, and surround the throne of God with a perpetual hymn.

The angels with their golden harps sing praises continually, and the cherubim fly on wings of fire.

This country is Heaven: it is the country of those that are good; and nothing that is wicked must enter there. (99–100)

With remarkable swiftness she passes over the negativity of animals, plants, and people who will not be chosen for this paradise.

The toad must not spit its venom amongst turtle doves; nor the poisonous henbane grow amongst sweet flowers. Neither must any one that doeth ill enter into that good land.

Her picture of heaven is all the more cheering because the forecasted reunion with dead parents and friends will be part of a larger faithful community, extending to patriarchs and prophets.

When our parents and friends die, and are laid in the cold ground, we see them no more; but there we shall embrace them again, and live with them and be separated no more.

There we shall meet all good men, whom we read of in holy books. There we shall see Abraham, the called of God, the father of the faithful; and Moses, after his long wanderings in the Arabian desert; and Elijah, the prophet of God; and Daniel, who escaped from the lions' den; and there the son of Jesse, the shepherd king, the sweet singer of Israel. They loved God on earth; they praised Him on earth; but in that country they will praise Him better and love Him more.

The appeal of this hymn lies in more than the continuing deictic contrast between here and there; it rests on the calm, assuring voice, the everyday statements which become philosophical propositions, and the blending of familial and biblical figures.

Allegories

Barbauld's paralleling of earthly and heavenly stories also introduces the third literary genre in which biblical narratives, characters, and motifs are prominent, the allegory. Mrs. Sherwood's *The Infant's Progress from the Valley of Destruction to Everlasting Glory* (1821) is a Bunyanesque redaction about the journey of three children from the Village of Family Love to the Celestial City. Their mentor and guide is Evangelist, who constantly inveighs against Mr. Worldly Prudence, Filthy Curiosity, and their ilk:

> These are the men . . . who think themselves wiser than their Maker, and who turn aside many young persons from the right way, in order to fill them with such knowledge as only puffeth up, and tendeth to destruction. They take the sling and the stone from the hand of the youthful pilgrim, and put on him the armour of Saul; they rob him of his Bible, and fill his mouth with the words of man's wisdom: so that more young pilgrims are destroyed by this *Worldly-Prudence*, than by thousands of the open enemies of our Lord. (23)

As well as upholding the Bible as the natural weapon against all personifications of worldliness, Sherwood's allegory is suffused with scriptural texts; through paraphrase, allusion, and, most often, direct quotations, the Authorized Version supplies the unabashed clichés of every conversation. Under the tutelage of the shepherd Sincerity the children concentrate on the scriptures, with the younger ones memorizing "certain portions" and the eldest reading passages "in the original languages" (52). The girls are six and eight years old; their brother is only ten. Yet the narrator "strictly require[s] of them all to take up their cross; to crucify the flesh with its affections and lusts" (47).

Grimness was still the salient feature of biblically inspired journey allegories a half century later. The author of *The Glorious City: An Allegory for Children* (1858), identified only as M.A.O., was imbued with a like fervor, as she plotted the journey of seven orphan-children—Stolz, Ernest, Wilfrid, Constance, Frivola, Debola, and Grace—along the Narrow Way, across the Rocky Valley and Dark River, and through the Gates of Pearl to the Happy City. The Stranger issues to each of the children a token, "a beautiful piece of polished ivory on which were engraved some deep crimson letters," and although only four of the seven reach the gate, M.A.O. alleviates any sense of mysterious fatality by appending almost one hundred pages of explanations. She defends her work as both an allegory and a parable, defining the first as "a tale or story that is intended to teach some lesson or truth beyond what the mere words express" (69) and the second as "an earthly story with a Heavenly meaning" (70). Biblical texts are cited to support every proposition: that the orphans represent "man's miserable condition" (Ps 51:5), that the tokens indicate "faith in the blood of Christ" (Eph 2:8), and that the cloaks symbolize "the perfect righteousness of Christ . . . which as a robe covers all their own imperfections" (Rom 3:22). She also wags an admonitory finger at the sins of the lost three:

> Stolz's sin was works without faith (Mark xvi.16). Frivola's was faith without works (James ii.14). And Wilfrid's was neglect of both faith and works (Psalms ix.17). (165)

One of the finest nineteenth century allegories, in my assessment, is concerned less with the journey metaphor and more with deft characterization within a domestic story disclosing a spiritual meaning. It is Mrs. Cameron's *The Baby and the Doll; or, Religion and Its Image* (1826), an account of the Christmas visit of two little girls to the home of young Charlotte Jesse. Anne and Myra are studies in contrast, between docility and tomboyishness, priggishness and bluntness. According to the advance notice of her father's letter, Anne is hardly a child at all:

> . . . her manners and behaviour are those of a woman. Really, I hardly know a fault she possesses, and she has everybody's good word. You would be astonished at the number of hymns and chapters she can say by heart; and she often tells me that she prefers learning these to any kind of play. (10)

If formality and appearance are important to one family, a different set of expectations, as outlined in the other parent's letter of introduction, reigns in Myra's home:

> My little Myra is not brought up in the modern school, and perhaps I have indulged her, since her mother's death, too much. I must prepare you, if you allow her to come, for

> expecting what in our days was called a Tomboy: but I trust
> she will not injure your little Charlotte; for, allowing for
> the partiality of a fond father, she certainly is a thoroughly
> affectionate, generous, good-hearted child. (14)

The girls' twelve day stay is educative all round. The pristine Miss
Jeffreys is immediately mesmerized by Charlotte's collections of
Mother Goose tales and pores over them—in private—mainly because, as she admits, "if they had been in our house . . . they would
have lighted the fire long ago" (25). But the consequences are
more public and revealing when Anne tries to shift the blame for
the broken dish and spilt barberry cream, the results of her pilfer-
ing, to the poor cat. This crisis of conscience opens up the allegorical meaning of the tale. Myra is quick to call Anne a hypocrite,
admitting proudly that she would have done the same thing as the
culprit and publicly, too, for, as she reasons, "I never set up for
being better than I am." It falls to Charlotte's guardian to set the
two visitors straight. Mr. Jesse attempts this delicate task by using
the difference between a doll and a baby to speak about "fake
religion [as] only an imitation of true religion" (58).

Dramas

The women who wrote biblical dramas for well-read and articulate children in general appealed to an older and more sophisti-
cated audience. While they were just as eager as the catechists,
versifiers, and allegorists to make their material "pleasant and prof-
itable," they also indulged in some remarkable interpretive liber-
ties, which I think parents highmindedly connived at in the inter-
ests of instruction. Or it might just be that the few women who
were creative or daring enough to make the attempt at biblical
drama were accepted and applauded on the basis of their reputa-
tion as teachers alone.

The best known French example is the Comtesse de Genlis'
seven-volume *Théâtre a l'Usage des Jeunes Personnes* (1785), the first
volume of which consisted of Sacred Dramas, which was made
available to English readers in Thomas Holcroft's translation by
1786. The countess' penchant for treacly melodrama is fully dis-
played in her version of "Ruth and Naomi" which she advertises as
"a masterly effusion of feeling and simplicity, and a precious monu-
ment of ancient manners" (219). The first exchange between Ruth
and Boaz, narrated in Ruth 2:8–14, offers no basis for Genlis' two

entirely fabricated scenes in which a charmed Boaz, displaying more than curiosity, is relieved to ferret out the information that she is "a widow, and so young!" and Ruth, "agitated" and "perplexed," coquettishly tries to stifle her own "strange sensations."

The sober counterbalance to this parlor entertainment is Hannah More's *Sacred Dramas* (1782), which, before publication, had been performed by students at the school in Bristol which More ran with her four sisters. Five blank-verse plays full of philosophic ruminations and grandly Miltonic phrases, they are a far cry from the jog-trot couplets of her Cheap Repository Tracts. Further, while her invented scenes, like those of the countess, explore interior action, they do so without the slightest hint of playing to the crowd or taking the Bible texts less than seriously. For example, although Saul's monologue from *David and Goliath* is not derived from any specific scene in 1 Samuel, it is a fitting and explanatory disquisition on the "evil spirit" (1 Sam 16:14) that troubled the king of Israel.

> Saul. WHY was I made king? what I have gain'd
> In envy'd greatness and uneasy pow'r,
> I've lost in peace of mind, in virtue lost!
> Why did deceitful transports fire my soul!
> When Samuel plac'd upon my youthful brow
> The crown of Israel? I had known content,
> Nay happiness, if happiness unmix'd
> To mortal man were known, had I still liv'd
> Among the humble tents of Benjamin.
> A shepherd's occupation was my joy,
> And every guiltless day was crown'd with peace
> But now, a sullen cloud forever hangs
> O'er the faint sunshine of my brightest hours,
> Dark'ning the golden promise of the morn.
> I ne'er shall taste the dear domestic joys
> My meanest subjects know. True, I have sons,
> Whose virtues would have charm'd a private man,
> And drawn down blessings on their humble sire.
> I love their virtues too; but 'tis a love
> Which jealousy has poison'd. Jonathan
> Is all a father's fondness could conceive
> Of amiable and good—Of that no more!
> . . .
> My subjects clamour at this tedious war,

> Yet of my num'rous arm'd chiefs not one
> Has courage to engage this man of Gath.
> O for a champion bold enough to face
> This giant-boaster, whose repeated threats
> Strike through my inmost soul! There was a time—
> Of that no more! I am not what I was.
> Should valiant Jonathan accept the challenge,
> 'Twould but increase his influence, raise his fame,
> And make the crown sit lightly on my brow.
> Ill could my wounded spirit brook the voice
> Of harsh comparison 'twixt sire and son. (Part III)

With similar earnestness in *Daniel*, More creates a seven-part drama from the mere mention of duplicity at the court of Darius (Dan 6:6), introducing two believable schemers, the Machiavellian Pharnaces and envious Soranus—reminiscent of the councillors of Pandemonium—and detailing with meticulous care their plot to undermine Daniel's "popular virtues and eclipsing merits" (102). The hero is a prophet, comforter, and catechist who, through biblical paraphrase and cross-reference, instructs his noble Median friend, Araspes (More's invented sounding-board). The unfolding action demonstrates how the king, as an admirer but also an administrator, is the man caught in the middle. The action itself is neither frenzied nor physical; cool psychology, moreover, is outmatched by "wonder-working" faith, a virtue Daniel attempts to explicate as beyond and above any philosophy:

> Enough to animate our faith, we know,
> But not enough to soothe the curious pride
> Of vain philosophy! Enough to cheer
> Our path we see, the rest is hid in clouds;
> And heaven's own shadows rest upon the view!
> (Part II)

The prophet's examples of faith in action, "eternal substance of our present hope . . . evidence of things invisible," are an appropriate catalogue of inherently weak and strong Old Testament figures.

> If I should tell what wonders Faith achiev'd
> By Gideon, Barak, and the holy seer,
> Elkanah's son; the pious Gileadite,
> Ill-fated Jephthah! He of Zorah too

In strength unequall'd; and the shepherd-king
Who vanquish'd Gath's fell giant! Need I tell
Of holy prophets, who by conqu'ring Faith,
Wrought deeds incredible to mortal sense;
Vanquish'd contending kingdoms, quell'd the rage
Of furious pestilence, extinguish'd fire!
Victorious Faith! others by thee endur'd
Exile, disgrace, captivity, and death!
Some uncomplaining, bore (nor be it deem'd
The meanest exercise of well-try'd Faith)
The cruel mocking, and the bitter taunt,
Foul obloquy, and undeserv'd reproach:
Despising shame, that death to human pride. (Part II)

There is no gruesome scene in the lion's den, only Daniel's confident resolve to turn "to the strong hold, the bulwark of [his] Strength, / Ready to hear, and mighty to redeem" (Part VII) and a single sentence about the bloody end of the plotting "wretched princess."

Stories

The most extensive and diverse biblical interpretations by women writers for children are found in their full-length stories, especially those of the golden age in the latter half of the nineteenth century. Unlike the conversational pose of proscription-filled catechisms, the rhyming see-saw of pious verses, the deliberate counterpointing of earthly and heavenly meanings in allegories, and the cardboard characterizations of most biblical drama, story telling called on all the descriptive resources of prose to create fully realized characters and gripping action that in itself subtly conveyed, illustrated, and commented on biblical dicta and pericopes. I have chosen what I think is a trio of the best and most distinctive styles, representing the adventure story through Charlotte Tucker, the call to reform through "Hesba Stretton" (Sarah Smith), and the pinnacle of narrative art through Juliana Horatia Ewing.

The outstanding practitioner of religious adventure was Charlotte Tucker, who wrote over a hundred intensely moral tales under the pseudonym of A.L.O.E. Set in every imaginable clime, her novels are stirring tributes to Christian fortitude under stress; two of them are actually set in Canada (which Tucker visited in 1857, before she embarked to India as a missionary volunteer). The trust in the scriptures shown by the teenaged orphan twins, Amy and Albert Gaveston, ensures their safety during all sorts of perils— the ravages of weather, the ferocity of wild bears, and the very real possibility of destitution—in *The Lake of the Woods: A Tale Illustrative of the Twelfth Chapter of Romans* (1867). Tucker's other Canadian novel, *Life in the White Bear's Den* (1884), relates the drastic changes in the life of a London socialite, Juliet Erle, after she is rescued from shipwreck and befriended by the Moravians in their Labrador mission at Eschol; although the sight of men in frock-coats and a woman in a scanty riding cape amid Labrador snow drifts is unintentionally amusing, A.L.O.E.'s story of a new-found shelter is really devoted to praise of the Moravians as a model biblical community. The wedding present this one-time heiress comes to prize the most is the Bible she receives from her Moravian future father-in-law.

By contrast, exactitude of setting is the hallmark of Hesba Stretton, whose stories of children alone in the slums of large industrial cities not only fueled the movement for health, education, and labor reforms but also showed a particular and individually-learned understanding of biblical precepts about charity. The children in Hesba Stretton's stories suffer from more than sickness, dislocation, and gossip; existence itself is a struggle for these waifs and city arabs. In *Pilgrim Street* (1867) Tom Haslam, with a father who is an idle ticket-of-leave man, endures his shabby life in the hope of helping his younger brother to an education. *Little Meg's Children* (1868) has a heroine who pawns her clothes to feed her younger sibs. *Alone in London* (1869) is the story of Tony, who sleeps in a box and spends his days sweeping passageways and running errands to help support Old Oliver and the man's granddaughter. Although the heroine of *Jessica's First Prayer* (1867) is neglected, abused, and abandoned by her drunken mother, the child sits in rapt attendance at chapel.

The very earnestness of their struggle for physical existence usually corresponds to a growing, experiential awareness of the spiritual life. Scavenging for food and shelter leads Stretton's waifs to a knowledge of grace and heaven. The places of her stories, rather than being the mere backdrops or platforms from which Christian principles are propounded, are actually the testing ground where they are shaped and learned. Readers must first feel the desolation and joylessness of Jessica's "home" before they can appreciate the surprise and mystery that this "little heathen"

(35) experiences in a Evangelical chapel. Stretton takes pains to convey the dehumanizing, animalistic nature of Jessica's existence as reflected in her dwelling:

> It was a single room, which had once been a hayloft over the stable of an old inn, now in use for two or three donkeys, the property of costermongers dwelling in the court about it. The mode of entrance was by a wooden ladder, whose rungs were crazy and broken, and which led up through a trap-door in the floor of the loft. The interior of the home was as desolate and comfortless as that of the stable below, with only a litter of straw for the bedding, and a few bricks and boards for furniture. Everything that could be pawned had disappeared long ago, and Jessica's mother often lamented that she could not thus dispose of her child. (28)

Although Stretton makes no bones about the pharisaism of the verger and many members of the congregation, she is also explicit about the awesome haven the church affords her "drudge and errand-girl" as early as Jessica's first visit; Stretton's description of this moment is based on the distinction between what the child has known and what she has just discovered:

> Thinking sadly of the light, and warmth, and music that were within the closed doors, she stepped out into the cold and darkness of the streets, and loitered homewards with a heavy heart. (38)

Of course not all the poor are benevolent, nor are all families secure. Stretton designs *Pilgrim Street* as a study in contrasts—between families, fathers, and brothers. Tom discovers the Bible through the warm hospitality of the Pendleburys. His own father, the ex-convict, presents such a contrast to Nat Pendlebury and to the Heavenly Father whom Tom is coming to know that the boy is continually remarking on the difference:

> "Father" had two sounds for Tom, one so full of gracious comfort, and of peace passing all understanding, that an hour ago he could not refrain from whispering it to himself over and over again. But the other sound was one of

shame, and misery, and dread, and his lips trembled
when he had to utter it aloud. Only an hour since his
heart had seemed full of music and singing, as he looked
up to the narrow strip of sky lying above the streets, and
said, "Father!" But now the word that had been like a tone
out of an angel's song had become a hateful and jarring
sound. (119–120)

Tom cannot persuade the sneering Haslam who taunts his son,
berating his new-found religion:

A fine father! . . . and thou't a nice one, to call God father! Does he know thou't ragged and clemmed? Why, I
serve the devil, and he's a better master. (134)

So unnatural and perverse is Haslam that he sets out to ruin his
younger, more impressionable son as a kind of sadistic vengeance.
His attempted arson at the mill precipitates the catastrophe and
brings about the final, fatal confrontation between Tom and his
father. In describing the boy's heroic effort to rescue Haslam,
Stretton emphasizes the differences between two types of vision.
While the trapped arsonist, "his eyes glaring with terror," stands
"fascinated and paralyzed . . . too bewildered to see that he could
himself reach the ladder by which his son was ascending," Tom
climbs the ladder alone, "his upturned face shining in the lurid
light with a strange smile upon it" (180–181). The fact that Tom
has forced his way on to the ladder with the proclamation "He is
my father, I tell thee . . . and he doesn't love God!" intensifies the
contrast between the light-hating madman and the illumined child.
    In the stories of Juliana Horatia Ewing dichotomies are less
pronounced; adventures are more domestic than exotic; and the
need for internal, personal reform supplants the call for social
transformation. But her stories are in no way a muted or dimin-
ished version of earlier work; they are exquisitely controlled minia-
tures whose narrative pattern appears to be easy and natural but is,
in fact, as carefully tended as the flowers and greenery Ewing
portrayed so fondly and often. Two works that are especially illustrative of her art as a story teller and allegorist are, in a sense,
extended botanical emblems. *Mary's Meadow* (1884) and *The Trinity
Flower* (1871) both deal with the cultivation of gardens as reflections and refinements of personality. *Mary's Meadow*, the story of a
child who plants seeds and cuttings in waste-places and hedges to

beautify them for travelers and who is frightened off by the churl-ish Squire barking at her for encroaching on his land, is, in one view, a straightforward tale of the old man's reformation. But it is also a story that subtly explores the connections between character and place, human development and seasonal growth. As the narra-tor, Mary explains how finding an old book in their library, John Parkinson's *Earthly Paradise, or Paradisi in sole Pardisus terrestris* (meaning, literally, "Park-in-sun's Earthly Paradise") gave her the idea of making "an Earthly Paradise of Mary's Meadow"; accord-ing to the child the plan emerged spontaneously: "Some books, generally grown-up ones, put things into your head with a sort of rush, and now it suddenly rushed into mine." Perhaps, the grown-up reader might conclude, the whole idea for *Mary's Meadow* came with a rush to Ewing after her reading of George Herbert's "The Flower," which she uses as the epigraph. The poet's surprise that his "shrivel'd heart" has "recover'd greenness" (lines 8–9), his de-sire to be "Fast in Thy Paradise, where no flower can wither" (line 23), and his evocation of humanity as "but flowers that glide" (line 44) were no doubt suggestive influences during the story's composi-tion. Just as Mary's attempt to create an earthly paradise has started the battle between her and the Squire, Ewing skillfully constructs their reconciliation scene around the Squire's gift of flowers and ultimately the meadow itself to Mary. The running heads of Ewing's tale provide a proverb-like shorthand. The epi-sode of Mary's discovering Parkinson is headed "God Almighty First Planted a Garden," while the eventual reconciliation unfolds under the banner, "Pardons and Pleasantness are Great Revenges of Slanders."

The narrator's surprise which closes *Mary's Meadow* contrasts with the predictable but nonetheless poignant ending of *The Trinity Flower*. This "legend" of a blind hermit's approaching death not only describes his garden and its medicinal plants with detail and beauty but it also spotlights the mystically threefold Trinity Flower to signal the old man's change from bitter resentment of his blind-ness to benign acceptance. This shift is most evident in his attitude toward the boy who, having once stolen crabapples from the her-mit's garden, begs to be allowed to help the old man whose sight and health are failing. Although the boy resolves to serve the her-mit, citing the biblical examples of Samuel and Timothy, the boy's persistence is only rewarded or recognized when the hermit relates his dream about the Trinity Flower and then proceeds to compli-ment the boy on three non-existent flowers in their garden and to utter this triadic refrain about his wished-for cure: "If God will. When God will. As God will." His death, movingly related by the descriptions of a vision declaring "I can see" and of the hermit's body stretched upon his pallet with the Trinity Flower in his hand, captures the two levels of this allegory with a final precision.

Just as *The Trinity Flower* is composed, appropriately, of various sets of three, *Daddy Darwin's Dovecot,* subtitled "A Country Tale," moves with the unhurried cadences of the "two gaffers gossiping, seated side by side upon a Yorkshire wall" and ostensibly serving as narrators. Probably influenced (I like to think in unprovable ways) by *Silas Marner,* it is the story of a miserly old bachelor's slow embrace of community, when he decides to take home a lad from the workhouse. A two-part flowering occurs: Daddy Darwin becomes a father and Jack March shows the true extent of his pluck and industry. Having grown up in a crowded vicarage herself, Ewing indulges in some genial satire of the Vicar's genteel, protected daughter, who invites the workhouse children to tea. But Jack's abject smarting about the gardener's false charges of theft against him brings this airy gesture of charity down to earth:

> Jack shared the terrier's mood. What were tea and plum-cake to him, when his pauper-breeding was so stamped upon him that the gardener was free to say—"A nice tale too! What's thou to do wi doves, and thou a work'us lad?"—and to take for granted that he would thieve and lie if he got the chance? (19)

Morality, Identity, and Justice

This practicality, exposition of hypocrisy, and rootedness in a knowledge of old and young people control *Daddy Darwin's Dovecot* in a way similar to the control of the Bible on the moral tradition of children's literature. The work of these women was intensely, proudly ideological. True, they wrote about constraints and about limitations of action based on these constraints. Their interpretations consisted of the use of biblical characters and texts in telling stories to educate their audience in a sense of virtue: the Bible was their ultimate measure and model. As managed with varying degrees of artistry and skill, narrativity was their way of understanding themselves and inculcating what they perceived to be fundamental principles. In defining man as "a teller of stories that aspire to truth," Alasdair MacIntyre comments on the blend of the unknown and the determined in our lives as in our stories:

> Unpredictability and teleology therefore co-exist as part of our lives; like characters in a fictional narrative we do not know what will happen next, but none the less our lives have a certain form which projects itself towards our future. (201)

The women who wrote for children in the eighteenth and nineteenth centuries would be the last to deprive them of stories, leaving them, according to MacIntyre, "unscripted, anxious stutterers in their actions as in their words" (201).

Modern readers and critics judge the script they provided to be narrowly doctrinaire and deterministic, predictably teleological. The most common reactions to them, often missing the subtle and implicit distinctiveness of the accomplishments of these women presenting religious and theological issues for children, are dismissiveness and neglect, or, worse, patronage. The women's grasp of life—their own and their readers'—impresses some as rigid and reductive. Their singular energy as pioneers in the moral education of the young, now held to be both unpopular and untenable as an occupation, is usually overlooked.

Rather than airbrushing these women out of the picture of cultural or literary history, we should accord them a finer and more expansive justice. Neither eccentric in their religious sensibilities nor incapable of posing questions and offering criticism, they realized acutely that morality and identity were two sides of the same coin. Of course, they were anything but value-neutral. Yet just as, in his latest book, Charles Taylor has exposed the fallacy of considering ourselves without or beyond frameworks, I think his engaging premise, that our sense of self is constituted in "a certain space of questions, as we seek and find an orientation to the good" (34), might provide a needed perspective on these neglected and undervalued women authors. Without resorting to the anger that MacIntyre sometimes vents against modernity's liberalism and individualism, Taylor conducts a generous and fair examination of all frameworks which "place us before an absolute question . . . framing the context in which we ask the relative questions about how near or far we are from the good" (45). The fact that the matriarchs and governesses of the moral tradition in children's literature asked their questions within a framework that may seem to us simplified and unproblematized could supply, according to Taylor's argument, sufficient grounds for disagreeing with them; however, it is not enough to discount or dismiss them.

A deeper exploration of motives, norms, and, where possible, consequences of this matriarchal moral tradition is needed. Two encouraging studies that could serve as standards are Anne Taves' characterization of mid-nineteenth century American Christianity, in *Household of Faith* (1986), and Marilyn Chapin Massey's examination of the fate of Friedrich Frobel's *Mutter- und Kose-Lieder* (Mother and Nurture Play Songs) in mid-nineteenth century Germany. Massey shows how "Mother Songs' religious symbols and metaphors, its maternal theology and reference to transcendence" (161), were precisely the features that caused it to be labeled subversive by the Prussian minister of education and unsafe by an American pedagogue. Taves speculates about gains and costs of the "implicit feminization" (210) of major devotional practices, and concludes that the stress on nurturing and the domestic sphere deserves "neither contempt nor glorification" (219). It is time to submit the early women authors of children's literature to the same well-balanced, unblinkered, and revealing scrutiny.

5

Feminist Hermeneutics
"An Ablative Estate"

If the root metaphor of Christianity is a particular kind of relationship between God and human beings, then it is an event, an alive, moving and changing occurrence which *no* metaphors or models can capture and pin down.
—Sallie McFague, *Metaphorical Theology*

Interpretation is necessarily a reader's response brought to a text; it is, at most, an interaction, at least, a purely subjective act.
—Mieke Bal, *Death and Dissymmetry*

Passages like the sacrifice of Isaac (Gen 22), Elijah on Mt. Horeb (I Kgs 19), and selected prophetic oracles (e.g. Isa 43:18f.; Jer 31:22) demonstrate that no particular statement of faith is final. Without rewriting the text to remove offensive language, feminism opposes, from within Scripture, efforts to absolutize imagery. The enterprise uses the witness of the Bible to subvert androcentric imagery.
—Phyllis Trible, "Five Loaves and Two Fishes: Feminist Hermeneutics and Biblical Theology"

Feminist hermeneutics allows for no fence-sitting: who is not for it is against it. The gaps separating its practitioners from the earlier interpreters seem more apparent than any linkages. Unlike the writing of medieval nuns, renaissance polemicists, and Georgian governesses, this undertaking is invariably more sociological and political than, strictly speaking, religious and devotional. Interrogating both the theological, sacramental orthodoxy so crucial to the medieval visionaries and the maintenance of a social order dear to the matriarchs and governesses, the enterprise does not subscribe to a truth that is single, imitable, and absolute, but to an understanding that is multiple, layered, and changing. Usually affiliated with the academy and publishing through university presses rather than associated with religious orders or promoted through tract societies' patronage, feminist interpreters expose and critique patriarchal privilege in biblical scholarship as well as liturgical practices to offer a new awareness of experience, to redress the balance, and to redefine order in human society. Theirs is a "hermeneutics of suspicion," in Elisabeth Schüssler Fiorenza's terms, which sometimes leads to a "hermeneutics of remembrance" ("Remembering," 57). Given the enormity of this task, it is natural to assume that opposition will be entrenched. Revived charges of heresy are often heard: Mary Daly has been tagged a neo-Gnostic and the inclusive-language lectionary, a new form of Docetism. Even though some interpreters are more polemical than others, the reader—as always, but especially so in the case of feminist hermeneutics—cannot remain a passive bystander. Engagement is all.

Hence, the irony of my confession: admitting the need to come up for air from revisionist theorizing, complaints about exclusion, and jeremiads against patriarchal misunderstanding might only establish me as faint-hearted. When the prose became angry and impenetrable, or solutions involving cooperation and mutuality seemed toothless, far-fetched, or saccharine, I would turn to poetry, specifically the work of Emily Dickinson. Drawn to statements about the "internal difference / Where the Meanings are" (#258), I kept seeing in Dickinson's "Bandaged moments" (#512) connections to and forecasts of the theory from which I was supposed to be taking a break. Her description of life and belief as "at best / An ablative estate" (#1741) captured for me the sense of taking away, separation from, and maybe even reduction of the scripture I was experiencing in contemporary interpretations. But Dickinson's poem also caught the energetic opposite charge or countervalence of the ablative estate in the desire to enlarge and increase.

> That it will never come again
> Is what makes life so sweet.
> Believing what we don't believe
> Does not exhilarate.

> That if it be, it be at best
> An ablative estate—
> This instigates an appetite
> Precisely opposite.

This mixture of ablation and addition is a suitably metaphoric depiction of feminist hermeneutics; the closing twist of change, difference, or meliorism nicely expresses its purpose.

As in all hermeneutic activity, an understanding of the creative and distorting potential of language is central to feminist work, two principal aspects of which I propose to discuss in this chapter. Rediscovering the traditional syncretism and reclaiming the imagery of the feminine divine not only cast Judeo-Christian monotheism in the light of surrounding polytheistic practices and mother goddess religions, they also promote a multi-dimensional view of God, blending maternal and paternal, practical and mystical, immanent and transcendent traits. In addition, feminist-inspired reformulations of lectionaries and examination of the assumptions inherent in biblical and theological scholarship strive to fashion language which includes and considers all of humanity.

Beyond God the Mother

Although, as Sandra Schneiders has pointed out, "theological tradition has never assigned sex to God" (3), gendered descriptions of divine power, majesty, and knowledge occur throughout the Bible. Moreover, although theologians claim that *Deus non est in genere,* the metaphors, symbols, and familial roles characterizing God in scripture all aid our faulty human perception of the *mysterium tremendum.* Feminism's reconsideration of the prominence of a whole set of cultural and linguistic paradigms in pre- and post-biblical literature acknowledging and revering woman—as not just mother and nurturer but as source of learning, sovereign, legislator, chastiser, and corrector—offers many surprising parallels to the Bible's pluriform depictions of God.

Stretching as far back as 25,000 B.C.E., the times of the non-nomadic Aurignacian mammoth hunters, to the closing of the last goddess temples in 500 C.E., the worship of a female divinity with women serving as clergy marked ritual practices throughout the immense Eurasian territories extending from southern France to Siberia. Bearing such titles as Sun Goddess, Mother Earth, Queen of Heaven, Valiant Warrior, Goddess of Intelligence and Knowledge, Directress of People, Prophetess, and Lady of Vision, the goddess was worshiped in societies where, as Merlin Stone affirms, "the earliest law, government, medicine, agriculture, architecture, metallurgy, wheeled vehicles, ceramics, textiles and written language were initially developed" (13). Decades before Stone's *The Paradise Papers,* Mary Esther Harding's Jungian study of religious concepts and symbols as manifestations of psychological attitudes, *Woman's Mysteries, Ancient and Modern,* was especially interested in the goddesses of love and fertility who, despite having several sexual partners, were nevertheless designated as virgins. Harding defines the virgin as belonging "to herself alone," being "one-in-herself" (79), which independence distinguishes these goddesses from other female deities created as the counterparts, extensions, wives of gods, a mere *syzygy* of the male. Whether with Jung, Harding, Erich Neumann, (*The Great Mother*), and Joan Engelsman (*The Feminine Dimension of the Divine*) we prefer to call independent action instances of the feminine archetype, or whether with Andrew Greeley (*The Mary Myth: Or the Femininity of God*) we prefer the label paradigm, it is necessary to recognize that greatness and terribleness can be combined in a single figure; as Erich Neumann sums up the "wreath of symbolic images" (12) surrounding the many figures within the archetypal feminine and combining positive and negative attributes, "sometimes the elementary and sometimes the transformative character is predominant" (38). Demaris Wehr's forthright study of the misogyny and fear of the feminine in Jung's "anima" sees fewer options. *Jung and Feminism* indicts the anima concept as a distortion of reality which soothes men's fears about, and encourages them to discover, the feminine side of themselves; Wehr argues for women's exploration of a positive animus which will no longer internalize or legitimate patriarchal society's "devaluation of women" (124), nor accept uncritically Jung's gender-related images dealing "primarily with the inner world of the male and its projections" (126).

Whatever the perspective or psychological slant, the inclusive—attractive and terrifying—roles of mother, maid, and anima are prominent features of ancient reliquiae. Maternal, regal, imperious characteristics, often accompanied by animal emblems like serpents and lions, are captured in the remaining figurines and friezes from the Gravettian-Aurignacian site and in Israel, Palestine, Crete, Syria, Italy, and Carthage.

Text and statuary together account for many of the claims and counter-claims about early Jewish ritual. Raphael Patai has examined the various feminine numina—Asherah, Astarte, Matronit, Shekinah, Cherubim, and Lilith—in Talmudic and midrashic sources, and concluded that their mixing of chastity and promiscuity, of motherliness and bloodthirstiness, reflects "the ambivalence of religio-sexual experience" (244). Although the scholar of Jewish mysticism, Gershom Scholem, makes it clear that Kabbalism is "both historically and metaphysically . . . a masculine doctrine, made for men and by men . . . free from the dangers entailed by the tendency towards hysterical extravagance" (37), and repudiates the idea that terms such as Princess, Matron, Queen, or Bride represent "a feminine element in God" (229), he does admit that "Kabbalism . . . was tempted to discover the mystery of sex within God" (235). Scholem's special concern is the sexual symbolism of the thirteenth century masterwork, the *Sefer ha-Zohar* (The Book of Splendor). The Zohar describes the ten sefiroth, spheres of divine manifestation, "mystical crowns," "King's faces," as "the ten stages on the inner world, through which God descends from the inmost recesses down to His revelation in the Shekinah" (214); since, as Scholem observes, "every true marriage is a symbolical realization of the union of God and the Shekinah" (235), it is not impossible to consider these divine symbols and manifestations as a combination of masculine and feminine attributes (Figure 3). The "garments of the Divinity" and elements of "a mystical organism" supply the Kabbalist, according to Scholem, "with a ready justification for the anthropomorphic mode of Scriptural expression" (214).

And yet Scholem insists on the masculine character of Kabbalism and its "inherent tendency to lay stress on the demonic nature of women and the feminine element of the cosmos" (37). Perhaps the reason for this insistence and for the simultaneous demise and fear of goddess worhip in earlier cultures is precisely, as Carol Christ has pinpointed it, the acknowledgement and dread "of the legitimacy of female power as a beneficent and independent power" (277).

Reactions hinting at dread and fear are also evident in the various reasons adduced for the demise of the goddess and the glossing over of the feminine attributes for the divine. Among them are the long periods of assimilation with Indo-Europeans, followed, from about 2400 B.C.E., by the victories of the pastoral, patriarchal, warlike, and expansive Indo-European invaders, whose reverence of Marduk, Ashur, Hor, and Ptah reduced the goddesses to secondary and often servile figures; later the influx of Hellenized Jews

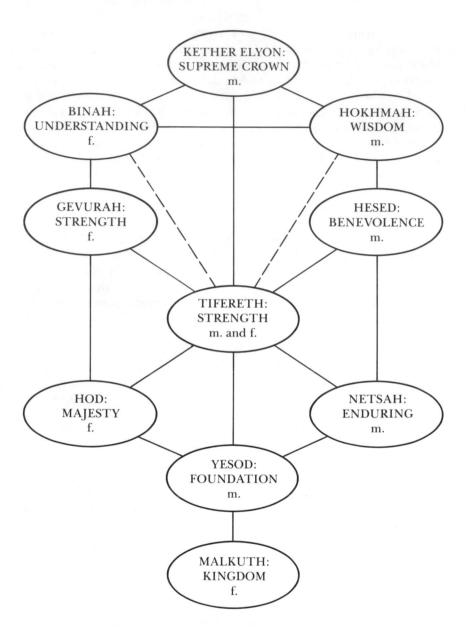

Figure 3.
The ten sefiroth ("spheres of divine manifestation") from the
Sefer ha-Zohar (The Book of Splendor). Note that Kabbalism alters
the grammatical conventions of gender.

into Christianity and Christianity's move from a lower to a middle class religion accounted for a further reduction of women's role and voice. Despite the abundance of gnostic texts in biblical and immediately post-biblical times, the split between orthodox and gnostic circles grew, as Elaine Pagels documents the case, because of the acceptance or rejection of "the principle of equality between men and women" (*Gnostic Gospels,* 79). Consequently the praise of equality and of the maternal nature of the Father in the second century *Paedagogus,* by the avowedly Christian and orthodox Clement of Alexandria, was an exceptional and a minority opinion but, for our purposes, one well worth hearing. Clement's nurturing God is simultaneously masculine and feminine:

> The food—that is, the Lord Jesus—that is, the Word of God, the Spirit made flesh, the heavenly flesh sanctified. The nutriment is the milk of the Father, by which alone we infants are nourished. . . . Hence seeking is called sucking; for to those babes that seek the Word, the Father's breasts of love supply milk. (I. 6)

The closing "Hymn to Christ the Saviour" pictures its subject endowed with breasts and dispensing the milk of the Word.

> O Christ Jesus, heavenly milk of the sweet breasts of the graces of the Bride, pressed out of Thy wisdom. Babes nourished with tender mouths, filled with the dewy spirit of the rational pap, let us sing together simple praises, true hymns to Christ [our] King, holy fee for the teaching of life. (III. 12)

Similarly surprising and heartening is his depiction of men and women sharing in perfection and receiving the same instruction and discipline. Clement denies the distinction between some baptized who are "illuminated" and others who remain "animal (or natural)," echoing the baptismal reunification formula of Galatians 3:28 to declare that "all who have abandoned the desires of the flesh are equal and spiritual before the Lord" (I. 6).

Reconsidering Eve

Clement's erudite plea actually reveals what were and continue to be two of the sorest points: the recognition of equality and of the rightness of desire. Challenging much of biblical rhetoric itself, mention of the principle of equality forces us to decide whether we agree with—vocally or tacitly—or dispute Qoholeth's embittered conclusion that a just woman is impossible to find: "one man among a thousand I found, but a woman among all these I have not found" (Eccl 7:28). Since many of the arguments of Clement's and our own contemporaries direct an accusing finger at woman in general and Eve in particular as temptress, mere helper, and after-thought, it is not really roundabout to ground a discussion of the feminine aspect of the creator in an examination of the first female.

By casting Eve in a new light, contemporary hermeneutics and semiotics are actually carrying on a long-standing tradition. In the early eighteenth century Mary Astell's *Reflections Upon Marriage* categorically dismissed the notion of women's inferiority. Positing that "a Rational Mind is too noble a Being to be Made for the Sake and Service of any Creature," Astell declared: " 'tis certainly no Arrogance in a Woman to conclude that she was made for the Service of GOD, and that this is her End" (Preface, A3). John Milton's Eve, who existed only for the God glimpsed in Adam ("He for God only, she for God in him," *Paradise Lost*, IV. 299), continues to provoke both apologetic and critical responses. While Diane McColley sees the Miltonic Eve as an autonomous artist, instilling in the reader "the arduous and joyful task of choosing and restoring goodness" (218), Mary Nyquist, by contrast, focuses on the issue that Eve's desire for another self and "novel female subjectivity" are essentially deemphasized, privatized, and sentimentalized: "throughout appropriated by a patriarchal order" (122). Though descriptively quaint by the modern standards of McColley and Nyquist, the exegesis of Elizabeth Cady Stanton is nonetheless a straightforward praise of Eve, who "appears to great advantage" (25). Stanton replays the Eden "drama" from the point of view of the woman in whom "the tempter . . . roused. . . . that intense thirst for knowledge, that the simple pleasures of picking flowers and talking with Adam did not satisfy" (25).

More recently, Phyllis Trible also praises Eve as "intelligent, informed, and perceptive. Theologian, ethicist, hermeneut, rabbi, she speaks with clarity and authority" (*Rhetoric*, 110). Trible bases her argument on a close examination of the Hebrew text. The fact that the nouns in Genesis 1:27, *hā'ādām*, humankind, and *zākār ûněqēvâ*, male and female, and their corresponding pronouns, *'ōtô*, him, and *'ōtām*, them, are all "objects of the verb *create* with God as its subject" (17), presents creation neither as androgynous nor as "an original unity split apart by sexual division," but as "the original unity that is at the same time the original differentiation" (18). The creation model is one of equality, not hierarchy. The grammatical gender of the earth creature (*hā'ādām*) does not constitute sexual identification. What is clear is that this sexually undifferentiated creature owes its existence to Yahweh who is also the consummate punster. With Adam's admission, "This at last is bone of my bones and flesh of my flesh; she shall be called Woman (*'iššâ*), because she was taken out of Man (*'iš*)" (Gen 2:23), he recalls the original word play of his own generation from the earth (*hā' ādām* from *hā'ădāmâ*) in the functionally parallel unit of *'iš* and *'iššâ*.

While Trible stresses unity, solidarity, and equality in her reading of the creation narrative, Mieke Bal concentrates on the semiotic principle of differentiation as "the main characteristic of the creation" ("Sexuality," 320). Taken from, differentiated from the earth, *hā'ādām* becomes a living creature (*nepeš*) thanks to Yahweh's breath. Turning her attention to the second account she observes that "it is *'iššâ* who changes the meaning of *hā'ādām* from earth being into earth man. In this semiotic sense, the woman was formed first, then the man (*contra* 'Paul')" (323). Though woman is the first to be signified, man, of course, is the first to speak and name, that is, to label the character in a way that completes its formation. About this final process of mutual creation through difference, Bal concludes:

> She was the first to be named, hence, to be "the other character" indispensable for him to be a character at all. Thus they mutually create each other, differently, in a different act. (336)

Yahweh the Mother

The stress on mutuality and difference, in contemporary feminist hermeneutics of the creation narratives, provides one form of introduction to the biblical imagery of the feminine divine. My point is not to suggest that the two millennia devoted to God the Father now must be followed with equal time for God the Mother, nor to imply that the similes, metaphors, and figurative language on the biblical texts are anything more than intimations, instances of Sinonimia, attempts to describe the numinous, awful, ineffable wholly Other. These attempts might fall on either side of the spectrum which Rudolph Otto has delineated. That is, they might be evidence of "the lowest and earliest level of the religion of primitive man, where the numinous consciousness is but an incohate stirring of the feelings . . . which often ends by constructing such a plausible fabric of interpretation, that the 'mystery' is frankly excluded" (26–27). Conversely they could be witnesses to the fact that "the truly 'mysterious' . . . is beyond our apprehension and comprehension . . . because in it we come upon something inherently 'wholly other' . . . before which we therefore recoil in a wonder that strikes us chill and numb" (28). But surely it is important to see in such human language, whether rationalizing or wondering, reflections of both creatures, the female and the male. Although we can probably cite quite readily a host of examples of sexual reversals and androgynous figures from myth and literature—including Hera's parthenogenetic birth of Athena, Zeus' carrying of Dionysus full term in his loin, Dante's use of Beatrice as a transformative anima and metaphor of Christ, Spenser's female knight Britomart, and even Milton's empowering Muse and "celestial Patroness" (*Paradise Lost,* IX. 21), Aphrodite-Urania, who "dictates to [him] slumb'ring, or inspires / Easy [his] unpremeditated Verse" (lines 23–24)—there has been no similar readiness, it seems to me, to acknowledge the maternal, domestic, and queenly aspects of God.

Yahweh the mother, groaning in labor, suckling and protecting children, and consoling them with divine reassurance, speaks often to Israel. God, who has kept silent, promises, in Isaiah 42:14, to cry like a woman in labor. The King James Version continues: "I will destroy and devour at once." The Hebrew, misrepresented in this translation, is actually an accurate and a rhythmic account of the cries and long and short breaths of a birth scene:

> *kayyôlēdâ 'ep'eh 'eššōm vě'ešap yāhad:* Like the woman about
> to bear a child, I cry out; I gasp and pant together.

The passage is all the more remarkable because it interrupts a figurative procession describing the Lord as "a man of war" (41:13), prevailing against his enemies, laying waste mountains and hills, and drying up herbs. While the Authorized Version continues the emphasis on martial prowess, the Hebrew text clearly combines creative and destructive aspects in its "new song" (41:10) unto the Lord. It is worthwhile, too, to locate this song of laboring creation and saving demolition within the context of First Isaiah's promise of the Lord of Host's defense and deliverance of Jerusalem (31:5) and Third Isaiah's consoling image of Jerusalem's abundant breasts, a metonymic picture of Yahweh's maternal care:

> For thus says the Lord: "Behold, I will extend prosperity to
> her like a river, and the wealth of the nations like an over-
> flowing stream; and you shall suck, you shall be carried
> upon her hip and dandled upon her knees. As one whom
> his mother comforts, so I will comfort you. (66:12–13)

Allusions to Yahweh's maternity serve frequently to remind heedless or forgetful children. Yahweh's charge to the unmindful people, in Deuteronomy 32:18, is that they have forgotten the Rock who begot them, the God who bore them; it is a fascinating combination of second-person singular masculine participial forms to describe male and female activities, fathering and bearing:

> ṣûr yĕlādĕkā teši vattiškah 'ēl mĕhōlălekā: You deserted the
> Rock who fathered you and forgot the God bearing you.

Individual voices confirm the integral role of Yahweh in their birth. More than a midwife, Yahweh is addressed by the psalmist as a figurative birth canal:

> 'attâ gōhî mibbāten: You are my breaking of waters from
> the womb. (Ps 22:9)

The life-giving waters are also prominent in Jeremiah's image of Yahweh as "the fountain of living waters" (2:13).

Yahweh's concern for the house of Jacob "since conception" (minnî beten) and "since birth" (minnî rāham) are reiterated often in prophetic literature:

> Hearken unto me, O house of Jacob, and all the remnant
> of the house of Israel, which are borne by me from the
> belly, which are carried from the womb. (Is 46:3)

Patriarch, psalmist, and apostle on occasion utilize this maternal image of the divine. When the wandering Israelites complain to Moses of their unchanging diet of milled and baked manna and remember fondly the fish, cucumbers, melons, leeks, onions, and garlic of Egypt, their guide resents the role of harried mother and throws up his arms to Yahweh in desperation:

Moses said to the Lord, "Why hast thou dealt ill with thy
servant? And why have I not found favor in thy sight, that
thou dost lay the burden of all this people upon me? Did I
conceive all this people? Did I bring them forth, that thou
shouldst say to me, 'Carry them in your bosom, *as a nurse
carries the sucking child.*' " (*ka'ăšer yiśśā' hā'ōmēn 'et hayyōnēq*)
(Num 11:12–13)

The Authorized Version translates *ka'ăšer yiśśā'* "as a nursing father." So beleaguered is Moses that he is actually at the point of
telling Yahweh not to abandon his divine maternal responsibilities.
In an entirely different mood of irenic contentment David addresses the Lord "like a child quieted at its mother's breast" (Ps
131:2); he likens his soul, the very work of God's breath, hand,
and, to follow the image pattern, womb, to a child being weaned:

kĕgāmul 'ălê 'immô kaggāmul 'ālai napšî
Like an infant being weaned with its mother
My soul is even as a weaning child to me.

Testing the faith of the community in Galatia, Paul, with characteristic boldness, appropriates the divine role of woman in labor to further Christian formation: "My little children, with whom I am again
in travail until Christ be formed in you" (Gal 4:19), he writes, to con-
vince his hearers that they are indeed "children of promise" (4.28).

Israel is a child, loved and consoled by Yahweh, as Hosea
("When Israel was a child, I loved him [11:1]) and Isaiah ("Rejoice . . . that you may suck and be satisfied with her consoling
breasts" [66:10–11]) attest. The prophet denies any perversity in
Yahweh's ministrations:

Shall I bring to the birth and not cause to bring forth?
says the Lord; shall I, who cause to bring forth, shut the
womb? says your God. (Is 66:9)

Yahweh is also a protective God, fluttering over the people like a
mother eagle (Deut 32:11) and gathering the children of Jerusalem together "as a hen gathers her brood under her wings" (Mt
23:37). This trusting covert of divine wings (Ps 61:4), the shadow-
ing refuge (Ps 57:1), prompted John Donne to meditate in one
sermon on the implications of the metaphor "*Sub umbra alarum,*
Under the Shadow of thy Wings" (110). Though he upholds the

meaning of the most frequently used scriptural names of God, "Elohim, and Adonai, and Jehovah," as assurances "of his Power to deliver us" (109), he sees in the metaphor of wings in the psalms "a Refreshing, a Respiration, a Conservation, a Consolation in all afflictions" (110). Donne does not use any feminine forms in his explication, yet his emphasis on a power that is restorative rather than martial, sustaining rather than destructive, leads to a particular and non-traditional understanding of power:

> That though God does not actually deliver us, nor actually destroy our enemies, yet if hee refresh us in the shadow of his Wings, if he maintains our subsistence (which is a religious Constancy) in him, this should not onely establish our patience, (for that is but halfe the worke) but it should also produce a joy, and rise to an exultation, which is our last circumstance, *Therefore in the shadow of thy wings, I will rejoice.* (111)

The related and ultimate depiction of Yahweh's feminine power is in the welcoming but reproving, generous but demanding, call of Wisdom (*hokhmah*). Since Wisdom declares that she was there (*šām 'ānî*) when the heavens were prepared (Prov 8:27), and that Yahweh founded the earth through her (Prov 3:19: *yhwh běhŏkmâ yāsad 'āres*), she herself is an intimate manifestation of God. In commenting on the importance of this image in the historical situation of post-exilic Israel, Claudia Camp observes that Wisdom's indirect authority, showing "the true power of brain over brawn," actually holds out "a viable hope for a new kind of 'power' defined in terms of faith rather than politics, and located in the home rather than in a national government" (281). When Wisdom calls aloud in the streets (Prov 1:20: *bārĕhōvôt tittēn qōlāh*) and raises her voice in the public squares, she becomes an instant threat to fools who hate knowledge (Prov 1.29: *kî šān'û dā'at*) and fear not Yahweh. But to those who heed, she offers an abundant promise of renewal and understanding: "I will pour out my thoughts to you; I will make my words known to you" (Prov 1:23).

Though excluded from the Protestant canon, the Greek text, Solomon's hymn to Wisdom, is an eloquent extension of the traditional encomia for this divine attribute; its praises of her authority, omnipotence, omniscience, and transcendence, entirely consonant with the perceptions of Wisdom literature in general, offer a stirring and poetic formulation of the activities of God as Wisdom.

For there is in her a spirit quick of understanding, holy,
Alone in kind, manifold,
Subtil, freely moving,
Clear in utterance, unpolluted,
Distinct, that cannot be harmed,
Loving what is good, keen, unhindered,
Beneficent, loving toward man,
Steadfast, sure, free from care,
All-powerful, all-surveying,
And penetrating through all spirits
That are quick of understanding, pure, subtil:
For wisdom is more mobile than any motion;
Yea, she pervades and penetrates all things by reason of her
    purenesss.
. . .
For she is an effulgence from everlasting light
And an unspotted mirror of the working of God,
And an image of his goodness.
And she, though but one, has power to do all things;
. . .
For she is fairer than the sun,
And above all constellations of the stars:
Being compared with light, she is found to be before it;
For to the light of day succeeds night,
But against wisdom evil does not prevail;
But she reaches from one end of the world to the other
    with full strength,
And orders all things well. (Wisdom of Solomon 7:22–8:1)

Despite the fact that many symbols of the Johannine ideology,
especially the "light of the world" (Jn 8:12) metaphor, are derived
from the Wisdom tradition, there was a concerted attempt in the
first century to delimit the power of Hokhmah-Sophia and incorporate it within the personified male figure of Logos. The prime
example of this repression of Sophia occurs in the works of Philo
Judaeus, whose antipathy toward the feminine as inferior and secondary is a repeated theme:

How, pray, can Wisdom, the daughter of God, be rightly
spoken of as a father? Is it because, while Wisdom's name
is feminine, her nature is manly? As indeed all the virtues
have women's titles, but powers and activities of consum-

mate men. For that which comes after God, even though it were chiefest of all other things, occupies a second place, and therefore was termed feminine to express its contrast with the Maker of the Universe who is masculine, and its affinity to everything else. *For pre-eminence always pertains to the masculine, and the feminine always comes short of and is lesser than it.*

Let us, then, pay no heed to the discrepancy in the gender of the words, and say that the daughter of God, even Wisdom, is not only masculine but father, sowing and begetting in souls aptness to learn, discipline, knowledge, sound sense and laudable actions. (*Fuga* 50–52)

The work of the Ante-Nicene fathers, as Joan Engelsman has pointed out, was an attempt to reinstate and recognize the Wisdom tradition of the feminine. In addition to Clement's images of the nurturing God and statement that "the male is Christ, the female is the Church" ("The Homily Ascribed to Clement"), Tertullian, writing "On Prayer," extended the figure of *Mater Ecclesia* to include *Mater Nostra:*

> *Ne mater quidem Ecclesia praeteritur. Si quidem in filio et patre mater recogniscitur, de qua constat et patris et filii nomen.* (*PL* I, 1154)

> Nor is even our Mother, the Church, passed by, if, that is, in the Father and the Son is recognized the Mother, from whom arises the name both of Father and Son. (*Ante-Nicene Fathers,* III, 682)

This queenly and generative image of God as Wisdom bears a strong resemblance to the later Christian iconography of the Madonna in majesty, the *sedes sapientiae* (Figure 4). Aware of the distinctions between *latria* and *hyperdulia,* I am not suggesting that Mary takes the place of or represents God. But it seems to me that there are significant parallels between the Romanesque "awesome cult image of the throne of wisdom" (Forsyth 56) with its stiff, hieratic poses and the depiction of God as Lady Wisdom and an omnipotent Mother. Furthermore, the paralleling of the statuary of Wisdom enthroned to pagan reliquiae highlights the larger issue of the relationship of the female manifestations of God in Judeo-Christian scripture to the mother goddess rituals of sur-

Figure 4.
Notre Dame la Brune from Saint-Pourçain-sur-Sioule, an example
of *sedes sapientiae* ("Throne of Wisdom") statuary.

rounding polytheistic cultures. After the declaration of Mary as
theotokos (mother of God) by the Council of Ephesus in 431, "this
pose dominated all others in Marian art" (Engelsman 126). While
in Carolingian times the appeal of the authoritative figure enthroned was ready-made, a deeply theological conviction also provided a suitable climate for the genesis of the *sedes sapientiae* statuary. As Ilene Forsyth explains, "the desire to render such figures as
Mary and Christ in freestanding form was induced by the desire to
make them experiential, an almost essential precondition for the
realization of their beneficence" (7). Similarly, while our post-
liberation era applauds and endorses the accomplishments of
women, the reclamation of the female imagery of the divine is
intended not as a replacement for paternalism and patriarchy but
as an indication of the impoverishment of theological language by
any attempt to delimit the divine as wholly male or wholly female.
Biblical metaphors and anthropomorphism do not serve the cause
of androgyny either, but they must (and do) reflect the fullness
and diversity of humanity.

One of the factors contributing to the development of the
Throne of Wisdom tradition was the survival of pagan mother-
goddess figures in the medieval west. Although the statuary often
met with clerical censure, as in Bernard of Angers' disdainful allusion to the St. Foy at Conques "as if it were a likeness of Venus or
Diana" (Forsyth 63), the similarities between the sketches and rem-
nants of pagan figurines and the Romanesque madonna are quite
remarkable. Consider how the tiny statuette of a mother and child
from Prunay-le-Gillon (Figure 5) actually anticipates the Romanesque pose and costume. Despite the fears of some contemporaries
about the violation of sacred texts, links must be made between pre-
Christian ritual and post-Christian investigation. The enthroned
figure is both august and immediate, a mixture of realism and perspective games: she holds a man-child, not a chubby infant; her
simple tunic and pleated overgarment, sometimes complimented
by mantle and cope, obviate the need for any additional or symbolic
attribute, for the sacerdotal nature of the priestly chasuble and
pallium is apparent. The images of the feminine divine are equally
palpable and undeniable. Yet, for some, this "new thing" (Trible,
"Gift," 271) of a woman compassing a man (Jer 31.22) is an
impermissible violation of the one, true God.

Some religious symbolists might balk at the mixture of female
and male attributes in God. Certain scholars maintain that the transcendent deity, oriented to infinity and the coming kingdom, is the

Figure 5.
Mother and Child, cast after a lost original from
Prunay-le-Gillon.

masculine type of religion, while the God who is near, oriented toward earth, life, generation, and the mysteries of death, is the feminine type. The Brazilian liberation theologian, Leonardo Boff, in his recent study *The Maternal Face of God*, calls the former type "eminently uranic" and the latter, "chthonic or telluric" (84). Admitting the existence and entrenchedness of these contrasts, he concentrates nevertheless on Mary as "the concrete, enfleshed symbol of what will transpire when the whole feminine, in every human being in a proportion proper to each, is brought to fulfillment" (253–254). Few theorists are as devotion-centered or faith-directed. Moreover, Boff's definition of gendered types and distinctions between farness and nearness, eschatology and experience, fuels a dichotomous, potentially combative perception where views of God might actually be pitted against one another.

Although my own intention is not to line up sides or assign battle positions, several ironies remain. Like it or not, the images of God which the Bible repeats most often and which most believers recognize are those of the protecting king, the jealous covenanter, and the inescapable, always judging Father:

> Know then in your heart that, as a man disciplines his son,
> the Lord your God disciplines you. (Deut 8:5)

With few exceptions, women as individuals in the Hebrew texts are rarely exemplars of independent, beneficent power. Even the touted courage of Judith and Esther, in which they use sexuality and beauty for the "conservation rather than enlargement of Israel" (Ochshorn 191), must be seen against the larger patrilineal and patriarchal background of their culture.

However, one of feminism's major accomplishments is both the critique of such a background and the amplification of the concept of ruling. The image of God, laboring for, feeding, and reassuring Israel, requiring love, obedience, and knowledge, is a powerful and corroborative indication of the feminine presence in divine activities. The texts challenge not only the smugness of patriarchy but the conventional blinkers of monotheism too. Our answer to the question, "Does belief in One God require belief in only one image of God?" (Engelsman 152), becomes crucial. Whether these metaphors prompt us to catalogue potential biblical "texts of triumph"—as in the civil disobedience of the midwives Shiprah and Puah (Ex 1:17), the articulate faith of the Syrophoenician woman (Mt 15:28), Lydia's helpfulness to Paul (Acts 16:11–

15) and the discipleship of Phoebe and Junia (Rom 16:1–7)—or whether they serve to remind us of the reflection of both sexes in biblical language, they might also provoke a recoil in wonder that the mystery of God transcends fatherhood and motherhood.

The Challenge of Liberating the Word

As interpreters feminists want to liberate and open up both the language of scholarship and the language of worship. Enunciating distinctions between the world of the text and that of the interpreter is as important for feminist hermeneuts as it had been for Schleiermacher and continues to be for Ricoeur. Phyllis Trible defines feminism succinctly as a hermeneutic which "interprets existence" through a focus on "gender and sex" and a recognition of "the multivalency of language" ("Loaves," 280, 292). As well, feminist investigations in the field of biblical studies make free use of models from the social sciences, with the understanding that "comparative cultural analysis occurs at the juncture between differences and similarities" (Osiek, "Handmaid," 277).

The modes of feminist interpretation are as varied as the operating premises of the interpreters themselves. Adela Yarbro Collins identifies the distinction between the fundamental message of scripture and its particular time-bound formulations as the central problem of interpretation; she concentrates on the exodus tradition, the teachings of Jesus, and the Pauline understanding of Christian freedom as the focal points of the message because they clarify, respectively, the event of liberation generating a sense of *communitas*, the elevation of the lowly over the well-to-do, and the Pauline "subordination of hierarchical distinctions to the bond of Christian solidarity" ("Inclusive," 369). Rebecca Chopp draws a clear but somewhat tendentious line between "theology proper" and the "pluralism of feminist theologies" (239–240); onto theology's abstract and unchanging essence of being she overlays feminism's view of experience as natural and historical, interconnective and plural. She borrows the term "abduction" (or "retroduction") from the pragmatists to explain the orientation of feminist theology "toward transformation of concrete experience" (249). The dangers of creating too sharp and exclusive a demarcation are evident in Drorah Setel's work on method, which itemizes "the use of dualistic categories, a concurrent stress on separation, and the failure to distinguish between reality and truth" as the characteristics of "patriarchal modes of thought" (37).

Bemoaning or exaggerating the differences between patriarchal and feminist modes simply perpetuates dualist categories and adversarial attitudes. The liberationist emphasis of Elisabeth Schüssler Fiorenza seems more positive and productive—notwithstanding my agreement with Rosemary Ruether's caution that Fiorenza's *ekklesia gynaikon* "threatens to become a gynecentric reversal of androcentric ecclesiology" ("Review," 141). Although Fiorenza "insists on a reconceptualization of our language" different from the paradigms of androcentric scholarship, she also calls for a study of the past to recover "its unfulfilled historical possibilities . . . to keep our future 'open' in the light of our . . . heritage and identity" ("Remembering," 55, 54).

Within the pluralism of feminist scholarship there are, as Carolyn Osiek has shown, at least five distinct hermeneutical alternatives: the rejectionist alternative, as exemplified in Mary Daly's writing, denies any saving grace in the Judeo-Christian legacy; the loyalist alternative which defends this legacy is prominent in Evelyn and Frank Stagg's *Woman in the World of Jesus* and John Otwell's *And Sarah Laughed;* the revisionist alternative, arguing that the patriarchal mold has been historically and not theologically determined, is clear in Phyllis Trible's first book, *God and the Rhetoric of Sexuality;* the sublimationist alternative, emphasizing the otherness of the feminine, is presented with less sentimentality in Joan Engelsman's *The Feminine Dimension of the Divine* than in Virginia Mollenkott's *The Divine Feminine;* the liberationist alternative, which, in its advocacy of a transformation of social orders, is of most interest to me, is best illustrated in the studies of Letty Russell, Rosemary Ruether, and Elisabeth Schüssler Fiorenza.

As well as the careful reexamination of the Genesis creation narratives, the other biblical text which is a frequent topic of feminist investigation—within and outside of theological circles—is Judges. In a variety of ways feminist readers make what David Tracy calls an "experiential demand" on the language of Judges, moving it away from a "language of negative oppression and positive justice to explicitly Christian language of social sin and authentic liberation" (374). In addition to Phyllis Trible's treatment of the concubine, in *Texts of Terror,* there is Jo Ann Hackett's strong case for the Deborah-Jael stories as "a very female piece of literature," describing the battle with the Canaanites "precisely from the perspectives of the women in the story" (32). Even though Deborah was not a biological mother, Cheryl Exum uses the lineaments of the account of this warrior-leader in Israel "as a critique of a patri-

archal culture that produced too few individual female leaders"
(85). Johanna Bos' contribution to a volume investigating "female
wit in a world of male power" views Jael's killing of Sisera as a
counter-type-scene to the betrothal type-scene, insisting that translations and commentaries have "exaggerated" Jael's "deceptive-
ness" (52). Mieke Bal devotes two powerful books to an indictment
of the androcentric scholarship about and the violence against
women in Judges. Retelling the raw butchery and horizontal scat-
tering of the rotting flesh of the concubine, or patrilocal wife, as an
anti-sacrifice, Bal concludes that, in this desacralized milieu, it is
the judges themselves who need to be judged.

The Language of Worship

The biblical texts used in worship have also come under close
and critical scrutiny. One of the most hotly debated experiments in
the imaginative reconstruction of meaning and authentic liberation is *An Inclusive-Language Lectionary*, which emerged from the
Task Force on Biblical Translation of the Division of Education and
Ministry of the National Council of the Churches of Christ in the
U.S.A. Beginning in 1983 and following the pattern of the three-
year liturgical cycle, these three volumes contain readings "based
on the Revised Standard Version . . . with the text revised primarily in those places where gender-specific or other exclusive language could be modified to reflect in English an inclusiveness of all
persons." "All modifications," so the Preface maintains, "are sup-
portable by the original Greek and Hebrew texts" (6). The members of the Inclusive-Language Lectionary Committee, on which
women and men had equal representation, have announced their
working premise in this fashion:

> All persons are equally loved, judged and accepted by
> God. This belief has been promoted by the church and
> has its roots in the origins of the Judaeo-Christian tradi-
> tion. Young and old, male and female, and persons of
> every racial, cultural and national background are in-
> cluded in the faith community. Basic to a sense of equality
> and inclusiveness is the recognition that God by nature
> transcends all human categories. God is more than male
> and female, and is more than can be described in histori-
> cally and culturally limiting terms. Words and language,

though inadequate and limited, are means by which we convey God's holiness and mystery. (5)

Among the experimental means the Lectionary uses are the translation of "Elohim," "Adonai," and "Yahweh" from the Hebrew Scriptures as "God," or "the Lord," or "the Sovereign [or Lord] God"; of "Kyrios" from the Greek New Testament as "sovereign," "Christ," "God," or "the Lord"; of "Abba" as "God the Father and Mother" (since according to the argument that "metaphor provides a new way of seeing . . . God is the Mother and Father of the Child who comes forth" [270]); and of the Revised Standard's "Son of man" as "the Human One," in the belief that this title is "open to the same nuances of interpretation allowed by . . . 'the Son of man' " (274). The Lectionary also features a deliberate inclusion of the names of women, as in the frequent mentions of the God and house "of Jacob, Rachel, and Leah" (Is 2:3, 5).

Since use of the Lectionary is voluntary, reaction has come mainly from those denouncing or applauding its appearance. Elizabeth Achtemeier inveighs against the "systematic attempt to remove sexuality from males and to impose sexuality on God" (242). Charging that "the work denies the fleshy reality of the Incarnation," she concludes, "Faith has become subservient to idealogy, scholarly honesty to current notions" (245). Martha Ann Kirk, by contrast, contends that "this experimentation with inclusivity" is needed to free ourselves from worship's "subliminal messages of sexism" (246, 249). In arguing that "Christ is not significant for being a *male* offspring of a *male* God," she observes: "The historical Jesus was male, but the risen Body of Christ is the fullness of all humanity, male and female" (250). While Achtemeier mounts a cogent and persuasive disputation (many of her criticisms about the original unpaginated format and references to Abraham as our father as well as to Sarah and Hagar as our mothers have resulted in changes in the 1986 Revised Edition of Readings for Year A), an unfortunate tendency to reduce or overstate, as I see it, mars both critiques. Achtemeier's isolation of faith from ideology, scholarly honesty from current notions, is loaded so as to deny or neglect the necessary interfusion of both and the fact that scholarship remains honest largely by taking into account current notions. Kirk's emotional argument, on the other hand, is built on shaky ideological foundations; conjectures about the fullness of all humanity in the risen body of Christ do sound like a new form of docetism, stressing the human to define or delimit the divine.

Robert Hurd and Alan Jones have both made illuminating and cautionary observations on inclusivity. Instead of inclusivity's "across-the-board reactive suppression of the masculine"—what he calls the "emasculative undertow"—Hurd promotes the approach of complementarity, which would rely on "unembarrassed affirmation of positive masculine images of God" and "images and forms of address which are not gender-bound" or patriarchal (400–402). Unfortunately Hurd does not spend enough time contemplating the Herculean task of cleansing most biblical images of their patriarchal associations before his heralded age of complementarity dawns. Despite his advocacy of inclusivity, Jones is most exercised by the distortions entailed in the current "ecclesiastical Star Wars" (43), which transform theology into neurosis, pathology, or self-justification. Though he encourages more efforts to retrieve images of the feminine divine and prefers the language of mutual discipleship and compassionate acceptance, he sees the present situation bleakly, picturing traditionalists and feminists "stranded on opposite sides of a vast ocean of self-pity and mutual recrimination" (43).

My own view, based only on a reading knowledge of these three volumes, is that, though the premise is unarguable, the method of adding to or tampering with texts is often regrettable, clumsy, and distorting. Extending gendered, biblical descriptions is not quite the same thing as a group deciding it will opt for the chair, chairperson, or chairman label, not is it similar to putting texts together and teasing arcane meanings out of them, as Derrida has done in *Glas,* by lining up side by side such an odd couple as Hegel and Genet. The anomaly of importing words to a text which has provided the language of worship and religious tradition, along with an unfathomable pool of allusions and influences, is that it disguises rather than reveals.

I propose to cite the same verse or verses from the King James Bible, the Revised Standard Version and An Inclusive-Language Lectionary to illustrate the problem. John's famous description of the inspiring, creative Logos closes with this statement about the incarnation (1:14):

> And the Word was made flesh, and dwelt among us (and we beheld his glory, the glory as of the only begotten of the Father) full of grace and truth. (KJB)

> And the Word became flesh and dwelt among us, full of
> grace and truth; we have beheld his glory, glory as of the
> only Son from the Father. (RSV)

> And the Word became flesh and dwelt among us, full of
> grace and truth; we have beheld the Word's glory, glory as
> of the only Child from God the Father and Mother. (I-LL)

Notwithstanding the Lectionary's removal of gender from the
child and the awkwardness of repetition, the most disturbing feature of this version for me is its presentation of a human generative model of parents (God the Father and Mother) to explain the
existence, after them, of the Child, Logos. The logic is skewed: the
Word who was before all creation, its cause, suddenly becomes its
product. This fanciful depiction of the incarnation, with its human
modeling, negates the divine, transcendent mystery of the Trinity.

The lapses—in theology and syntax—are more apparent in
apocalyptic warnings and eschatological visions. After Jesus' observation about heaven and earth passing away and his words not
passing away, there follows this caution (Mt 24:36, 44) about
preparedness:

> But of that day and hour knoweth no man, no, not the
> angels of heaven, but the Father only. . . . Therefore be ye
> ready: for in such an hour as ye think not the Son of man
> cometh. (KJB)

> But of that day and hour no one knows, not even the
> angels of heaven, nor the Son, but the Father only. . . .
> Therefore you also must be ready; for the Son of man is
> coming at an hour you do not expect. (RSV)

> But of that day and hour no one knows, not even the
> angels of heaven, nor God's Child, but God only. . . .
> Therefore you also must be ready; for the Human One is
> coming at an hour you do not expect. (I-LL)

The twenty-fourth chapter of Matthew's gospel is full of ominous
forecasts, about "the end of the world" (24:3) in general and specifically about the destruction of the temple in Jerusalem, deliv-
ered by Jesus to his disciples on the Mount of Olives. He is close to
doubting their abilities to comprehend that "iniquity shall abound"

(24:12) and to be undeceived by false Christs and prophets. Hence, the urgency of his warning about end times is all the more poignant. The Greek text does not warrant the Revised Standard's addition of "nor the Son" ("nor the Son, but the Father only"), and so the Lectionary's attribution of ignorance to "God's Child" is also faulty. But more distressing, in my view, is the Lectionary's lessening of the real and purposeful terror (whether we like to acknowledge it or not) of a divine judge who will reward the wise and punish the wicked. The label "Human One" does not convey this august, deliberately more-than-human power.

The Lectionary's shifts in language might appear to be slight, but they have far-reaching theological consequences. It is more than a matter of conventional versus modern readings to refer to God as king, or ruler. The twenty-fourth Psalm praises the king of glory, *melek hakkabod*, four times; this king is described as "the Lord strong and mighty, the Lord mighty in battle" (v. 8). When the Lectionary replaces all references to "king" (*melek*) with "ruler" (*salit* being an entirely different word in Hebrew which does not appear in these biblical texts), it alters fundamentally the concept of divine kingship; the O.E.D. definitions of "ruler" include "one who, or that which, exercises rule, command, or authority" and, more tellingly, "one who has control, management, or headship within some limited sphere." The decision, apparently dictated by the use of "ruler," to refer to the "realm of heaven" (Year A, 20) rather than the "kingdom of heaven" relies on a slim or non-existent semantic difference; the O.E.D. lists "kingdom" and specifically "the kingdom of heaven" as the first two meanings of "realm." I am not unaware of the Lectionary Committee's desire to mitigate a stress on maleness, but adding to or changing texts in these ways— courageous eisegesis as it is—does not seem to me to be the most persuasive or defensible way of changing many attitudes.

Another, lesser-known experiment with inclusive language which suffers from no awkwardness or inconsistency is the version of the psalter prepared by Nancy Schreck and Maureen Leach, *Psalms Anew*. The language is direct and accurate, in no way diminishing the power of the original and often clarifying the ornate diction of the Authorized Version. The contrasts between human and divine goodness which inform all of Psalm 36 are sometimes lost in the embroidery of the King James Bible:

> The transgressions of the wicked saith within my heart,
> that there is no fear of God before his eyes. . . . Thy

mercy, O Lord, is in the heavens; and thy faithfulness reacheth unto the clouds. . . . They shall be abundantly satisfied with the fatness of thy house; and thou shalt make them drink of the river of thy pleasures. (verses 1, 5, 8)

Schreck and Leach translate simply, distinguishing the selfish depths of sin from the immeasurable expanse and welcoming hospitality of divine love:

Sin speaks to sinners in the depths of their hearts. No awe of God is before their eyes. . . . Your love, Yahweh, reaches to the heaven; your faithfulness to the skies. . . . They feast on the riches of your house; they drink from the stream of your delight.

Their translation of Yahweh's sheltering refuge makes divine protection a real and understandable asylum from human cruelty. The Authorized Version refers to the Lord hiding "them in the secret of thy presence from the pride of man" and keeping "them secretly in a pavilion from the strife of tongues" (31:20), but *Psalms Anew* fashions this practical, simple, yet poetic description:

Safe in your presence you hide them far from devious human plots; inside your tent you shelter them far from the battle of tongues.

Of course there are times when the grandeur of the King James Bible—no doubt a great part of which is its emotive, allusive appeal—is inimitable and unalterable, as in the opening of the Miserere:

Have mercy upon me, O God, according to thy lovingkindness: according unto the multitude of thy tender mercies blot out my transgressions. (51:1)

The simple translation, "In your goodness, O God, have mercy on me; with gentleness wipe away my faults," not only misses the chiastic structure but fails to capture the quivering plea of the creature.

A terse three-sentence Preface alerts the reader to the translators' commitment to inclusive language "so as to guard the authenticity of the Psalms while at the same time freeing them from their patriarchal bias." I found none of the additions of female names intrusive or puzzling. *Psalms Anew* brought to my mind Marjorie Proctor-Smith's concise analysis of "liturgical anamnesis": "to remember one's past is to have a future" (408). As a matter of fact, the inclusive language versions, as I hope the following side-by-side examples illustrate, cause us to recall the pivotal roles of these women in the stories and families to which the verses allude.

Thou hast with thine arm redeemed thy people, the sons of Jacob and Joseph. (77:15)	With your strong arm you redeemed your people, the descendants of Jacob and Rachel.
Thou leddest thy people like a flock by the hand of Moses and Aaron. (77:20)	You guide your people like a flock of sheep under the hand of Moses, Aaron and Miriam.
O Lord God of hosts, hear my prayer: give ear, O God of Jacob. (84:8)	Yahweh Sabaoth, hear my prayer; listen God of Jacob and Rebekah.
O ye seed of Abraham his servant, ye children of Jacob his chosen. (105:6)	Descendants of Abraham and Sarah, God's servants, offspring of Jacob and Rachel, God's chosen ones.
Which covenant he made with Abraham, and his oath unto Isaac. (105:9)	The pact made with Abraham and Sarah, the oath to Isaac and Rebekah.

Women in Biblical Texts and Worshiping Communities

One evident distinction between Schleiermacher's nineteenth century theory and contemporary hermeneutics is the latter's insistent blending of universal-objective "grammatical" interpretations with particular-subjective "psychological" interpretations. Such blendings are clear not only in the creative expansion of proper name formulae in inclusive-language versions but also in the arguments, supported by biblical narrative, about the place of women in Judaic and early Christian societies. In examining "female strategy" in the Jacob cycle, specifically the stratagems of Tamar, the widow of Judah's eldest son Er, Nelly Furman concludes that women whose role is "strictly biological . . . have no say in this male-marked genealogy" (113). Considering the literary characterizations of mothers in the Hebrew Bible—Sarah, Rachel, Leah, and Hannah, among them—in annunciation type-scenes and narratives about significant births leads Esther Fuchs to a claim about the narrow role of the mother-figure within the "patriarchal framework . . . its androcentric perspective confin[ing] her to a limited literary role, largely subordinated to the biblical male protagonists" (136). More recently Fuchs argues that gender is a primary factor in determining the literary presentation of deception in biblical narrative; she concludes that "an awareness of the interdependency of heterosexual politics and biblical narrative is the first step in the feminist critique of the patriarchal claim to absolute 'objective' truth" (82). Seen from the perspective of this scholarship and its mounted evidence, the addition of women's names in inclusive-language readings appears long overdue.

Historical criticism of Christian origins also affords a new understanding of the kingdom of God as designedly more than a male preserve. Elisabeth Schüssler Fiorenza concentrates on the heroism of Judith and the dramatic victory of wisdom over brute power "as a mirror image of Israel's situation under Roman occupation" (*Memory*, 118). Although proponents of the rejectionist alternative might only deplore the fact that this defeat is effected by Judith's sexuality and beauty, Fiorenza chooses to emphasize the triumph of mind over body, wisdom over power. The image of this strong and successful woman, Fiorenza argues, is a welcome counterbalance to the negative terms applied "to Jewish women of the first century in particular, and Jewish theology in general" (118). It helps, too, to assess the atmosphere in which Jesus preached of the kingdom not as the restoration of the Davidic sovereignty (however exaggerated claims of its influence might be) nor as the abolition of Roman colonialism, but as the discipleship of equals. "Jesus stresses that, in his own ministry and movement, the eschatological salvation and wholeness of Israel as the elect people of God is already experientially available: 'the *basileia* of God is in the midst of you' (Luke 17:21)" (119). His eating with outcasts and sinners, his healing of the sick and the ritually unclean, his breaking of the sabbath, and inversion of first and last indicate that the *basileia* vision is not a holiness of the elect. Not residing solely in temple and torah, this kingdom is open to all.

As for the "a-familial ethos" of the Jesus movement in Palestine, where house, brothers, sisters, mothers, fathers, children, lands, and, in the Lucan account, wives are to be left behind for the kingdom, Fiorenza pays careful attention to the synoptic texts and notes the singularity of the redaction in Luke. She proves that the responsible yet radical *basileia* vision appealed not only to a group of "itinerant charismatic men" (145) but to a new familial community where mothers and sisters figure prominently.

> Jesus is "inside" the house, "at home" (cf. Mark 3:19). He points to those who 'sat around him' and declares them to be his true family (v. 34). The discipleship community abolishes the claim of the patriarchal family. (147)

New Models of the Divine-Human Relationship

Current work in metaphorical theology also promotes new social models. Sub-titling her study "models of God in religious language," Sallie McFague focuses on personal and relational metaphors to explain how this "open-ended theology" realizes "the relativity of all models of the divine-human relationship and, with this sensibility, [is] ready both to question traditional models and entertain new possibilities which may overcome the limitations of present models" (161). Influenced by and indebted to Ricoeur, she believes that "reality is redescribed through metaphor" (40). They both prize conceptual language, which can preserve "the *tensive* character of symbolic language" (Ricoeur, "Hermeneutics," 36), and are equally absorbed in the theological task of interpreting "the primary language of a tradition with fresh possibilities for its becoming a transforming reality in our lives" (McFague 120).

A deliberate mixture of theology and fabulation, McFague's work is unified not in its concern with past and present stories but in its speculation about future possibilities. Rather than change or adapt biblical language itself, McFague is more interested in changing the ways of understanding and the emphasis in this language. Metaphor is, after all, "ordinary language," and "metaphorical thinking constitutes the basis of human thought and language" (15, 16). Therefore, in considering the most common Old Testament metaphors to describe God, as king, judge, husband, and master, McFague chooses to put less emphasis on the hierarchical nature of these images and stresses instead their personal and relational nature. The relationship between God and human beings is central to her thesis because this connection "disorients conventional standards and expectations and reorients us to a new way of being in the world" (177).

McFague uses a combination of Old Testament metaphor and the less direct, more extravagant language of the New Testament to advance the central model of God the friend. To the critical experiences expressed through the parental model (rebirth, nurture, unmerited love, security in God alone, compassion, forgiveness, service) she adds the balance of the model of the friend, which demonstrates mutuality, cooperation, and reciprocity. This move toward egalitarianism and immanentalism in the view of God, who is alongside rather than above us, is still difficult for me to accept completely because the divine, however compassionate, understanding, and near, remains, for me, mysteriously other and transcendent. This does not mean that I reject metaphorical theology. On the contrary, McFague's search for an accessible model has caused me to question many rote-learned catechetical assumptions and to become even more aware of the divide separating the homogenous theology of the medieval mystics as well as the family-based didacticism of the Georgian and Victorian governesses from the literalism and doubt of today's consciousness of the relativity and plurality of interpretations.

Horizons of Possibilities

These are very grand and sweeping claims indeed from one who admits not being a theologian. Yet concentrating on women authors and interpreters and appreciating the range, subtlety, and daring of their writing have made me less apologetic about the undertaking and more bold in its defense. More than anything else this investigation has convinced me of the multiplicity, particularity, and time-boundedness of interpretation. Not only in their dissatisfaction with authoritarian pronouncements but also in their revisionist interpretations of Judeo-Christian patriarchy, feminist hermeneuts are among the most bracing and productive of contemporary theorists. True, they question the stability of texts as repositories of absolute meaning; but they do not look at texts as mere allegories of their own unreadability, nor do they allow the open-endedness of textual indeterminacy to close down any critical forum. Their writing is deeply purposive in its presentation of new paradigms and blendings.

It seems a truism to remark that point of view is crucial, but it is precisely the importance of women's experiences, voices, and narratives to which feminist hermeneuts are drawing attention. Their questions in some ways echo Alice of Bath's query, "Who painted the leon, tel me who?" She in turn is repeating the question of Aesop's lion, when shown a picture of a man killing a lion. The suggestion is that the animal would represent matters differently, and Alice makes no bones about the sort of Book of Wicked Husbands female writers could produce:

> By God, if wommen hadden writen stories,
> As clerkes han within hir oratories,
> They wolde han writen of men more wikkednesse
> Than al the merk of Adam may redresse.
> ("Wife of Bath's Prologue," lines 699–702)

The replacement of literary misogyny with misandry is not the issue of feminist interpretations. Rather, the most promising studies promote mutuality, equality, and collaboration.

My own interest in this feminist work is its blending of hermeneutics, theology and literary criticism and theory, which I like to label a New Heterodoxy. I was attracted initially (perversely, some would say) to the civil agreement to disagree among theologians, Hebrew and Greek scholars, and feminist theorists. It may sound oversimplified, or reflect on the observer, to refer to biblical scholarship being carried on in such discrete fields. And, clearly, it would be naive to wish for greater collaboration among them without recognizing that the perspective of faith of some writers affects and colors their work substantially. What I am talking about is more than the dilemma of discussing the Bible as a literary, cultural, or historical document, and even more than the problems which professors of English may face when they are assigned to teach a course in the King James Bible. Yet my attraction to the topic of women's interpretations of the Bible has been due in part to these very problems. Rather than attempt to smooth out or ignore these differences, I have found that the jostling of disciplinary and religious and secular approaches is a creative friction, one that will not rewrite the Bible, but will surely continue to unsettle the smugness of centuries-old assumptions.

In a review of two Bibles for children released for the Christmas market, one a translation by Lore Segal and the other a series of Blake-inspired illustrations to the King James text, Mary Gordon provides a modern variant on Coleridge's confession about the Bible, that he was "unable to determine" what he did "not owe to its influences" (9).

> Reading a child the story of Moses and the burning bush is a qualitatively different act from showing him or her a Renoir or playing him or her the "Jupiter" Symphony. The whole process of reading Bible stories has a *charge*— one way or the other—which is why so many of them are pressed between covers for children and their anxious, guilty parents. (55)

Feminist interpreters understand the anxiety, might quibble about the guilt, and are keenly aware of the qualitative difference. Such an awareness explains the point and urgency of their suggested subtexts, alternate readings, and radical revisions.

Conclusion

Over four centuries ago Montaigne, in his essay "On Experience" (Book III, Chapter 13), observed that it was more important to interpret interpretations than to interpret things. Today's scholarship accentuates the point. In this meta-interpretive undertaking we, like Eliot's Prufrock, find that there is time for "a hundred visions and revisions," as we inch toward any understanding. Meanings, construals, interpretations continue to shift and slide, to elude our grasp. The more certain and firm our reading of a text becomes, the more likely it is that we have constructed such assurances by muffling questions, doubts, and revaluations. The essential indeterminacy of meaning in post-modern culture makes the activity of interpreting more complex and, possibly, more confounding than in any previous period.

It was this sense of the peculiarity and enormity of the task facing feminist interpreters of the Bible that first set me thinking about the earlier and fundamentally different contexts in which women have read and commented on the scriptures. And now, as I look back on the diversity of their accomplishments, I am struck by the fact that this anthology of anthologies—repository of faith and allusion for some and cultural artifact for others—has itself been shaped into a different text by each generation or age of female interpreters. For medieval holy women it was a guide, both allegorical and practical, for the perception of life, the conduct of liturgies, and the hope of eternal vindication. For renaissance exegetes it offered a platform for speaking out and a solid foundation on which to base their assertions or criticisms of belief. The women who used biblical characters and events as a way of instructing children transformed their source into a series of purposive narratives. Feminist inquirers return to this influential text, the origin of so many pernicious misconceptions about women as well as many unexamined praises of their strength and capacity, with a twofold

154

aim: to question and refashion the way things have been and are. Their work remains the most controversial of all because it interrogates the ideal of truth as single and normative, which underpins the previous interpretations of nuns, polemicists, and matriarchs.

The contexts for examining along with the views of the text itself have changed radically. Although it has hopscotched over centuries and countries, leaving untouched great periods of women's missionary work, especially in the new world, the foregoing selective sampling of women's interpretations has tried to let the works speak for their own authors and times. However, it is always a tricky business to present the material of other eras with a sympathetic willingness to understand what the society was like and without condescending or distorting judgments based on our current cultural expectations.

Despite the differences and distances, I firmly believe that there is a reason and a benefit in exploring what unites these women and not merely pointing out what separates them. Occasionally I indulge in creating a fanciful picture of a means of bringing them all together. As much as I respect and admire the individual qualities of each voice, I also consider cueing these voices for entry into a large and changing score. Imagine this ongoing choral work opening with the harmonic and rhythmic speech of the early medieval nuns, followed by chants and a gradually unfolding chant melisma when the tertiaries, beguines, and anchoresses add to their ranks. As the renaissance exegetes enter, contrapuntal choral structures take over; two sections can be engaged in dramatic colloquy with opportunities for fugues, arias, and arioso-like recitatives. The matriarchs and governesses, at first in formal unison, begin with elementary étude material, and then smaller groups pursue what appear to be improvisations, actually organized and settled forms, in marches, scherzos, rondos, and variations. While the rest of the chorus remains silent for the initial percussive sounds and atonal polyphonies of the feminists, the others eventually join in the truncated melodies, augmenting harmonies and providing a simple theme to be explored, reworked, and put back together again differently.

Though the choral metaphor joining voices across several centuries might seem far-fetched, it nevertheless indicates one of my underlying ideas. Feminist hermeneutics, while clearly not derived from women's earlier exegeses, gains a special resonance by being heard as part of the continuous and reformative enterprise of women's interpretive activity.

Notes

Chapter One

1. "Oration on the Dignity of Man," trans. E.L. Forbes, in *The Renaissance Philosophy of Man,* ed. E. Cassirer, et al. (University of Chicago Press, 1948), p. 223.

2. Wilhelm Dilthey, *The Understanding of Other Persons and Their Life-Expressions,* in *The Hermeneutics Reader,* ed. Kurt Mueller-Vollmer (New York: Continuum, 1989), p. 162.

3. White is quoting J.C.F. Schiller.

Chapter Two

1. As quoted by Caroline Walker Bynum, *Jesus as Mother: Studies in the Spirituality of the High Middle Ages* (Berkeley: University of California Press, 1982), p. 136.

2. As quoted by Joan Evans, *Life in Medieval France* (London: Phaidon, 1925, rpt. 1957, 1969), p. 120. The translation is my own.

3. As quoted by Joan Ferrante, *Woman as Image in Medieval Literature from the Twelfth Century to Dante* (New York: Columbia University Press, 1975), p. 6.

4. Katharina M. Wilson, trans., *The Dramas of Hrotsvit of Gandersheim* (Saskatoon: Peregrina Publishing, 1985), p. 25. Latin quotations from Hrotsvitha are based on *Hrotsvithae Opera,* ed. Helene Homeyer (Munich, Paderborn, Vienna: Verlag Ferdinand Schoningh, 1970). Vulgate quotations are based on *Biblia Sacra* (Matriti: Biblioteca de Autores Cristianos, 1959).

5. Three English translations of Hrotsvitha's plays are available: the colloquial, discursive prose of St. Jean (1923), the accurate, rhythmic prose of Bonfante (1979), and the terse, rhymed prose of Wilson (1985). In citing Homeyer's edition of the Latin text, with

scene and section numbers copied from von Winterfeld's 1902 edition, I have supplied my own translations and occasionally cited Wilson's.

6. As commentators have noted, the richly colored illustrations from Hildegard's visionary treatise, *Scivias*, in which a sketch of the *Ordo virtutum* forms part of the last vision, and especially the pictures of the virtues, provide some indication of the splendid vestments which might have solemnized the liturgical presentation in the convent at Bingen.

Both Hozeski, in *Annuale Mediaevale* (1978), and Dronke, in *Poetic Individuality* (180–192), have reproduced the Latin text of the play; Hozeski provides an English translation at the same time, while Dronke's translation appears in the booklet accompanying the record (1982) and compact disc (1987), *Hildegard von Bingen: Ordo virtutum*, Sequentia, dir. Klaus Neumann, Harmonia mundi 20395/ 96. I cite Dronke's Latin text and supply my own translations.

7. "Piety and stylistic expression are also a question of learning." See Margot Schmidt, " 'minne du gewaltige kellerin': On the Nature of *minne* in Mechthild of Magdeburg's *fliessendes licht der gottheit*," *Vox Benedictina* 4.2 (1987): 123.

8. See Gertrud Jaron Lewis, trans., "The Mystical *Jubilus:* An Example from Gertrud of Helfta (1256–1302)," *Vox Benedictina* 1.4 (1984): 237–247.

Chapter Three

1. The *Ten Articles* (1536) retained a belief in the real presence, although the term transubstantiation was not used; in fact, this belief was still taught in *The Necessary Doctrine and Erudition for Any Christian Man* (1543) which, because of Henry's precise, theological revisions, was often called *The King's Book*. It was only in the formulation of the Thirty-Nine Articles (1533), in Article XXVIII in particular, that transubstantiation was denied. See E.J. Bicknell, *A Theological Introduction to the Thirty-Nine Articles of the Church of England* (London: Longmans, Green and Co., 1919; rpt. 1955), pp. 8–9, 382.

Chapter Four

1. "A Memoir of the Author's Life," *Sacred Dramas*, Nineteenth Edition (London: William Milner, 1844), p. xvii.

Works Cited

Biblical Texts and Commentaries

Alter, Robert and Frank Kermode, eds. *The Literary Guide to the Bible*. Cambridge: Harvard UP, 1987.

Biblia Sacra, logicis partitionibus aliisque subsidiis ornata a R. P. A. Colugna et L. Turrado. Matriti: Biblioteca de Autores Cristianos, 1959.

Brown, Raymond E., S.S. and J.A. Fitzmeyer, S.J., Roland E. Murphy, O. Carm., editors. *The Jerome Biblical Commentary*. Englewood Cliffs: Prentice Hall, 1968.

Buttrick, George, et al., eds. *The Interpreter's Bible*. Twelve Volumes. Nashville: Abingdon Press, 1952–57.

———. *The Interpreter's Dictionary of the Bible*. 4 vols. Nashville: Abingdon Press, 1962.

Charles, R.H., editor. *The Apocrypha and Pseudepigrapha of the Old Testament in English*. London: Oxford UP, 1913.

Charlesworth, James H., ed. and trans. *The Odes of Solomon*. London: Oxford UP, 1973.

Crim, Keith, editor. *The Interpreter's Dictionary of the Bible*. Supplementary Volume. Nashville: Abingdon Press, 1976.

Green, Jay P., editor. *The Interlinear Bible*. Grand Rapids: Baker Book House, 1976.

The Holy Bible. Authorized Version. New York: Oxford UP, 1952.

The Holy Bible. Revised Standard Version. New York: T. Nelson, 1952.

Kohlenberger, John R., ed. *The NIV Interlinear Hebrew-English Old Testament*. 4 vols. Grand Rapids: Zondervan Publishing House, 1979.

Migne, J.-P. *Patrologiae Cursus Completus Series Latina*. Tunholti, Belgium: Typographi Brepols Editores Pontificii, 1857–1866.

Robinson, James M., ed. *The Nag Hammadi Library in English*. New York: Harper & Row, 1977.

Stanton, Elizabeth Cady, editor. *The Woman's Bible*. Reprinted Seattle: Coalition Task Force on Women and Religion, 1974.

Studies, Articles, and Reviews

The Account of the Sufferings of Anne Askew, Written by Herself, and reprinted by a Catholic. London: F. and J. Rivington, 1849.

Achtemeier, Elizabeth. "The Translator's Dilemma: Inclusive Language." *The Living Light* 22.3 (1986): 242–45.

Ackrill, J.L., trans. *De Interpretatione* in *The Complete Works of Aristotle*. Ed. J. Barnes. Princeton: Princeton UP, 1984.

Adams, Hazard. "Canons: Literary Criteria / Power Criteria." *Critical Inquiry* 15 (1988): 748–764.

Adey, Lionel. "Class-Conditioning in Nineteenth-Century Hymnals for Children." *Mosaic* 18 (1985): 87–99.

Adler, Ruth. "Rereading Eve and Other Women: The Bible in a Women's Studies Course." *Approaches to Teaching the Hebrew Bible as Literature in Translation*. Ed. B.N. Olshen and Y.S. Feldman. New York: MLA, 1989. 93–97.

Allen, Philip Schugler. "The Mediaeval Mimus." *Modern Philology* 8 (1910): 17–30.

Allen, Prudence. *The Concept of Woman: The Aristotelian Revolution (750 B.C.–1250 A.D.)*. Montreal: Eden Press, 1985.

Aquinas, Saint Thomas. *Summa Theologica*. 3 vols. New York: Renziger Bros. Inc., 1948.

Astell, Mary. *Reflections Upon Marriage, The Third Edition To Which is Added A Preface, in Answer to some Objections*. London, 1706

Atkinson, Clarissa, Constance Buchanan, Margaret Miles, eds. *Immaculate and Powerful: The Female in Sacred Image and Social Reality*. Boston: Beacon Press, 1985.

Saint Augustin's Christian Doctrine. Trans. J.F. Shaw. *A Select Library of the Nicene and Post-Nicene Fathers*. Ed. P. Schaff. Vol. 2. 1898. Reprinted Grand Rapids: W.B. Eerdmans, 1983.

Bal, Mieke. "Sexuality, Sin, and Sorrow: The Emergence of Female Character (A Reading of Genesis 1–3)." *The Female Body in Western Culture, Contemporary Perspectives*. Ed. S.R. Suleiman. Cambridge: Harvard UP, 1986. 317–338.

———. "The Bible as Literature: A Critical Escape." *Diacritics* 16 (1986): 71–79.

————. *Lethal Love; Feminist Literary Readings of Biblical Love Stories.* Bloomington: Indiana UP, 1987.

————. *Death and Dissymmetry: The Politics of Coherence in the Book of Judges.* Chicago: U of Chicago P, 1988.

————. *Murder and Difference; Gender, Genre, and Scholarship on Sisera's Death.* Trans. M. Gumpart. Bloomington: Indiana UP, 1988.

————. "Tricky Thematics." *Semeia* 42 (1988): 133–155.

Barbauld, Mrs. Anna. *Hymns in Prose for Children.* London: John Murray, 1880.

Beilin, Elaine V. *Redeeming Eve: Women Writers of the English Renaissance.* Princeton: Princeton UP, 1987.

Berger, Pamela. *The Goddess Obscured: Transformation of the Grain Protectress from Goddess to Saint.* Boston: Beacon Press, 1985.

Berrigan, Joseph R. "A Lovely and Useful Instruction by Angela Da Foligno." *Vox Benedictina* 2 (1985): 24–41.

Bicknell, E.J. *A Theological Introduction to the Thirty-Nine Articles of the Church of England.* 1919. London: Longmans, 1955.

Boehme, Jacob. *On the Incarnation of Jesus Christ.* Trans. J. Sparrow. 1647. Reprinted London: John Watkins, 1909.

————. *Mysterium Magnum.* Trans. J. Sparrow. 1654. Reprinted London: John Watkins, 1924.

————. *The Way to Christ.* Trans. Peter Erb. New York: Paulist, 1978.

Boff, Leonardo. *The Maternal Face of God.* Trans. R. Barr and J. Diercksmeier. San Francisco: Harper & Row, 1987.

Bonfante, Larissa, trans. *The Plays of Hrotsvitha von Gandersheim.* New York: New York UP, 1979.

Bos, Johanna W. H. "Out of the Shadows: Genesis 38; Judges 4.17–22; Ruth 3." *Semeia* 42 (1988): 37–67.

Brabazon, James. *Dorothy Sayers: The Life of a Courageous Woman.* London: Gollancz, 1981.

Brennan, Margaret. "Enclosure: Institutionalizing the Invisibility of Women in Ecclesiastical Communities." *Women—Invisible in Theology and Church.* Ed. E.S. Fiorenza and M. Collins. Edinburgh: T. & T. Clark, 1985. 38–48.

Brenner, Athalya. *The Israelite Woman: Social Role and Literary Type in Biblical Narrative.* Sheffield: JSOT, 1985.

Brinton, Howard. *The Mystic Will Based on a Study of the Philosophy of Jacob Boehme.* London: George Allen & Unwin, 1931.

Brown, Judith C. *Immodest Acts: The Life of a Lesbian Nun in Renaissance Italy.* New York: Oxford UP, 1986.

Bugge, John. *Virginitas: An Essay in the History of a Medieval Ideal.* The Hague: Martinus Nijhoff, 1975.

Bunyan, John. *A Book for Boys and Girls; or, Country Rhymes for Children.* London: Printed for N. P. and sold by the Booksellers, 1686.

Butler, Marguerite. *Hrotsvitha: The Theatricality of Her Plays.* New York: Philosophical Library, 1976.

Butler, Samuel. *Ernest Pontifex; or, The Way of All Flesh.* Ed. D.F. Howard. Boston: Houghton Mifflin, 1964.

Bynum, Caroline Walker. *Jesus as Mother: Studies in the Spirituality of the High Middle Ages.* Berkeley: U of California P, 1982.

———. *Holy Feast and Holy Fast; The Religious Significance of Food to Medieval Women.* Berkeley: U of California P, 1987.

Cameron, Lucy Lyttleton (Butts). *The Baby and the Doll, or Religion and Its Image.* London: Houlston and Wright, 1860.

Camp, Claudia V. *Wisdom and the Feminine in the Book of Proverbs.* Sheffield: JSOT, 1985.

Chamberlain, David. "Musical Learning and Dramatic Action in Hrotsvit's *Pafnutius.*" *SP* 77 (1980): 319–343.

Chopp, Rebecca. "Feminism's Theological Pragmatics: A Social Naturalism of Women's Experience." *The Journal of Religion* 67 (1987): 239–256.

Christ, Carol and Judith Plaskow, eds. *Womanspirit Rising: A Feminist Reader in Religion.* San Francisco: Harper & Row, 1979.

Christ, Carol P. "Reflections on the Initiation of an American Woman Scholar into the Symbols and Rituals of the Ancient Goddesses." *Journal of Feminist Studies in Religion.* 3 (1987): 57–66.

Saint Chrysostom: On the Priesthood. Trans. W.R.W. Stephens. *A Select Library of Nicene and Post-Nicene Fathers.* Ed. P. Schaff. Vol. 9. 1898. Reprinted Grand Rapids, W. B. Eerdmans, 1983.

Clark, Elizabeth, tr. *The Life of Melania the Younger.* New York and Toronto: Edwin Mellen, 1984.

———. *Ascetic Piety and Women's Faith; Essays on Late Ancient Christianity.* Lewiston: Edwin Mellen, 1986.

Clement of Alexandria: The Protreptikos. The Ante-Nicene Fathers. Eds. Alexander Roberts and James Donaldson. Vol. 2. New York: Charles Scribner's Sons, 1903.

Coffman, George R. "A New Approach to Medieval Latin Drama." *Modern Philology* 22 (1925): 230–71.

Cohn, Albert. *Shakespeare in Germany in the Sixteenth and Seventeenth Centuries.* 1865. Reprinted New York: Haskell House, 1971.

Coleridge, Samuel Taylor. *Confessions of an Inquiring Spirit.* Boston: J. Munroe, 1841.

Colledge, Edmund and James Walsh, trans. *Julian of Norwich. Showings.* New York: Paulist Press, 1978.

Collins, Adela Yarbro. "An Inclusive Biblical Anthropology." *Theology Today* 34 (1978): 358–69.

———. ed. *Feminist Perspectives on Biblical Scholarship.* Chico: Scholars Press, 1985.

Coulter, Cornelia. "The Terentian Comedies of a Tenth Century Nun." *Classical Journal* 24 (1929): 515–29.

Dalby, Mrs. Thomas. *Dutch Tiles: Being Narratives of Holy Scripture.* London: John Mason, 1842.

Daly, Mary. *Beyond God the Father; Toward a Philosophy of Women's Liberation.* Boston: Beacon Press, 1973.

———. *Gyn/Ecology: The Metaethics of Radical Feminism.* Boston: Beacon Press, 1978.

Devlin, Dennis. "Feminine Lay Piety in the High Middle Ages: The Beguines." *Medieval Religious Women: Distant Echoes.* Eds. J.A. Nichols and L.T. Shank. Kalamazoo: Cistercian Publications, 1984. 183–96.

Dickens, Charles. *Bleak House.* London: Chapman & Hall, n.d.

———. *Dealings with the Firm of Dombey and Son, Wholesale, Retail & for Exportation.* London: Chapman & Hall, 1894.

———. *The Personal History of David Copperfield.* London: Chapman & Hall, 1896.

Dronke, Peter. *Poetic Individuality in the Middle Ages: New Departures in Poetry 100–1150.* Oxford: Clarendon, 1970.

———. *Fabula: Explorations into the Uses of Myth in Medieval Platonism.* Leiden: E.J. Brill, 1974.

———. *Women Writers of the Middle Ages: A Critical Study of Texts from Perpetua (+203) to Marguerite Porete (+1310).* Cambridge: Cambridge UP, 1984.

Eckenstein, Lina. *Women Under Monasticism.* Cambridge: Cambridge UP, 1896.

Edgeworth, Maria. *Little Plays for Young People: Warranted Harmless.* 1827. London: Baldwin & Cradock, 1834.

Elkins, Sharon K. *Holy Women of Twelfth-Century England.* Chapel Hill: U North Carolina P, 1988.

Engelsman, Joan. *The Feminine Dimension of the Divine.* Philadelphia: Westminster Press, 1979.

Ewing, Juliana Horatia. *Daddy Darwin's Dovecot: A Country Tale.* London: S.P.C.K., 1884.

————. *Mary's Meadow.* London: S.P.C.K., 1886.

————. *Dandelion Clocks and Other Tales.* London: S.P.C.K., 1887.

Exum, J. Cheryl. " 'Mother in Israel': A Familiar Story Reconsidered." *Feminist Interpretation of the Bible.* Ed. L. Russell. Philadelphia: Westminster, 1985. 73–85.

Ferrante, Joan M. *Woman as Image in Medieval Literature from the Twelfth Century to Dante.* New York: Columbia UP, 1975.

Fiorenza, Elisabeth Schüssler. *In Memory of Her: A Feminist Reconstruction of Christian Origins.* New York: Crossroad, 1983.

————. *Bread Not Stone: The Challenge of Feminist Biblical Interpretation.* Boston: Beacon Press, 1984.

————. "Remembering the Past in Creating the Future: Historical-Critical Scholarship and Feminist Biblical Interpretation." *Feminist Perspectives on Biblical Scholarship.* Ed. A.Y. Collins. Chico: Scholars Press, 1985. 43–64.

Fiorenza, Elisabeth Schüssler and Mary Collins, eds. *Women—Invisible in Theology and Church.* Edinburgh: T. & T. Clark, 1985.

Flanagan, Sabina. *Hildegard of Bingen: A Visionary Life.* London: Routledge, 1989.

Forsyth, Ilene. *The Throne of Wisdom: Wood Sculptures of the Madonna in Romanesque France.* Princeton: Princeton UP, 1972.

Frankforter, Daniel. "Hrotvitha von Gandersheim and the Destiny of Women." *The Historian* 41 (1979): 295–314.

————. "Sexism and the Search for the Thematic Structure of the Plays of Hrotvitha of Gandersheim." *International Journal of Women's Studies* 2 (1979): 221–32.

Fuchs, Esther. "The Literary Characterization of Mothers and Sexual Politics in the Hebrew Bible." *Feminist Perspectives on Biblical Scholarship.* Ed. A.Y. Collins. Chico: Scholars Press, 1985. 117–136.

————. " 'For I have the way of women': Deception, Gender, and Ideology in Biblical Narrative." *Semeia* 42 (1988): 68–83.

Furman, Nelly. "His Story Versus Her Story: Male Genealogy and Female Strategy in the Jacob Cycle." *Feminist Perspectives on Biblical Scholarship.* Ed. A.Y. Collins. Chico: Scholars Press, 1985. 107–116.

Gatty, Margaret. *Parables from Nature.* First Series. London: George Bell, 1890.

Genlis, Stéphanie, comtesse de. *Sacred Dramas.* Trans. T. Holcroft. London: G.G.J. & J. Robinson, 1786.

Gerson, Jean. *De examinatione doctrinam, Joannis Gersonii . . . omnia opera.* Ed. L. Ellies-Dupin. 5 vols. Antwerp, 1706.

Gilder, Rosamond. "Hrotsvitha, The Strong Voice of Gandersheim." *Theatre Arts Monthly* 14 (1930): 331–44.

———. *Enter the Actress: The First Women in the Theatre.* New York: Theatre Art Books, 1931.

Ginzburg, Carlo. *The Cheese and the Worms.* Trans. J. and A. Tedeschi. Baltimore: Johns Hopkins UP, 1980.

Gordon, Mary. "The Word for Children." *New York Times Book Review.* 8 November 1987: 29, 55.

Gosse, Edmund. *Father and Son: A Study of Two Temperaments.* Ed. J. Hepburn. London: Oxford UP, 1974.

Grant, Barbara. "Five Liturgical Songs by Hildegard von Bingen (1098–1179)." *Signs* 5 (1980): 557–67.

Hackett, Jo Ann. "In the Days of Jael: Reclaiming the History of Women in Ancient Israel." *Immaculate and Powerful.* Eds. C. Atkinson et al. Boston: Beacon Press, 1985. 15–38.

Hadewijch: The Complete Works. Trans. Mother Colomba Hart. New York: Paulist Press, 1980.

Haight, Anne Lyon, ed. *Hrosvitha of Gandersheim: Her Life, Times, and Works, and a Comprehensive Bibliography.* New York: The Hrosvitha Club, 1965.

Halligan, Theresa A., ed. *The Booke of Gostlye Grace of Mechtild of Hackeborn.* Toronto: Pontifical Institute of Mediaeval Studies, 1979.

Happ, Howard J. "Theological Table-Talk: The Beauty of the Bible." *Theology Today* 40 (1984): 437–43.

Harding, Mary Esther. *Woman's Mysteries Ancient and Modern.* London: Longmans, Green, 1936.

Heine, Susanne. *Women and Early Christianity: Are the Feminist Scholars Right?* Trans. J. Bowden. London: SCM, 1987.

Hensley, Jeannine, ed. *The Works of Anne Bradstreet.* Cambridge: Belknap P, 1967.

Herminjard, Aimé-Louis, éditeur. *Correspondance des Réformateurs Dans Les Pays de Langue Française.* Tome Cinquième. Génève: H. Georg, 1874.

Heyward, Isabel Carter. *The Redemption of God: A Theology of Mutual Relation.* Washington: U of America P, 1982.

Hildebrant, Franz, ed. *A Collection of Hymns for the Use of the People Called Methodists. The Works of John Wesley.* Vol. 7. Oxford: Clarendon, 1983.

Hildegard of Bingen's Book of Divine Works. Ed. Matthew Fox. Santa Fe: Bear, 1987.

Hildegard of Bingen's Scivias. Trans. Bruce Hozeski. Santa Fe: Bear, 1986.

Hill, Rowland. *Divine Hymns Attempted in Easy Language for the Use of Children.* London: T. Wilkins, 1790.

Hindman, Sandra L. *Christine de Pizan's 'Epistre Othea': Painting and Politics at the Court of Charles VI.* Toronto: Pontifical Institute of Mediaeval Studies, 1986.

Hirst, Desirée. *Hidden Riches; Traditional Symbolism from the Renaissance to Blake.* London: Eyre & Spottiswode, 1964.

Homeyer, Helene, ed. *Hrotsvithae Opera.* Munich, Paderborn, Vienna: Verlag Ferdinand Schoningh, 1970.

Hosmer, Rachel. *Gender and God: Love and Desire in Christian Spirituality.* New York: Cowley, 1986.

Hozeski, Bruce. "The Parallel Patterns in Hrotsvitha of Gandersheim, A Tenth Century German Playwright, and in Hildegard of Bingen, A Twelfth Century German Playwright." *Annuale Mediaevale* 18 (1977): 42–53.

———. "*Ordo Virtutum:* Hildegard of Bingen's Liturgical Morality Play." *Annuale Mediaevale* 19 (1978): 45–69.

Hourlier, Jacques et Albert Schmitt, traducteurs. *Gertrude d'Helfta, Oeuvres Spirituelles, Texte Latin.* Paris: Les Editions du Cerf, 1967.

Howard, John. "The German Mystic Mechthild of Magdeburg." *Medieval Women Writers.* Ed. K. Wilson. Athens: U Georgia P, 1984. 153–85.

Hurd, R.L. "Complementarity: A Proposal for Liturgical Language." *Worship* 61 (1987): 386–405.

An Inclusive-Language Lectionary. Readings for Year A, Year B, Year C. New York: Pilgrim Press, 1984–86.

Inge, William R. *Studies of English Mystics: St. Margaret's Lectures, 1905.* London: Longmans, Green, 1907.

Jackson, Mary V. *Engines of Instruction, Mischief, and Magic: Children's Literature in England from Its Beginnings to 1839.* Lincoln: U of Nebraska P, 1989.

James, William. *The Varieties of Religious Experience: A Study in Human Nature.* London: Macmillan, 1902.

Jay, Nancy. "Sacrifice as Remedy for Having Been Born of Woman." *Immaculate and Powerful.* Ed. C. Atkinson et al. Boston: Beacon Press, 1985. 283–309.

Jenkins, Timothy. "Review Article: Janet Martin Soskice *Metaphor and Religious Language.*" *Literature and Theology* 3 (1989): 219–230.

The Principal Works of Saint Jerome: Letters, Treatises, Prefaces. Trans. W.H. Fremantle. *A Select Library of Nicene and Post-Nicene Fathers.* Second Series. Eds. P. Schaff and H. Wace. Vol. 6. 1903. Reprinted Grand Rapids: W.B. Eerdmans, 1983.

Johnson, Thomas H., ed. *The Complete Poems of Emily Dickinson.* Boston: Little, Brown, 1951.

Jones, Alan W. "Men, Women and Sex: Make Way for the Image of God!" *Worship* 62 (1988): 25–44.

Jones, Charles C. *The St. Nicholas Liturgy.* Berkeley: U of California P, 1963.

Jowett, Benjamin. *Scripture and Truth.* London: Henry Froude, 1907.

Kelly, Gary. "Romantic Evangelicalism: Religion, Social Conflict, and Literary Form in Legh Richmond's *Annals of the Poor.*" *English Studies in Canada* 16 (1990): 165–186.

Kieckhefer, Richard. *Unquiet Souls: Fourteenth-Century Saints and Their Religious Milieu.* Chicago: U of Chicago P, 1984.

Kilner, Dorothy. *The First Principles of Religion, and the Existence of a Deity, Explained in a Series of Dialogues Adapted to the Capacity of the Infant Mind.* London: John Marshall, 1787.

Kilner, Mary Ann. *Jemima Placid; or, The Advantage of Good-Nature, Exemplified in a Variety of Incidents.* London: John Marshall, 1783.

Kirk, Martha Ann. "Inclusive Language: A Pentecostal Event." *The Living Light* 22 (1986): 245–57.

Klemm, David E. *The Hermeneutical Theory of Paul Ricoeur.* Lewisburg: Bucknell UP, 1983.

Korshin, Paul J. "Queuing and Waiting: The Apocalypse in England 1660–1750." *The Apocalypse in English Renaissance Thought and Literature.* Eds. C.A. Patrides and J. Wittreich. Ithaca: Cornell UP, 1984. 240–65.

Kraft, Kent. "Hildegard of Bingen Three Songs." *Vox Benedictina* 1 (1984): 157–61.

———. "Five Songs by Hildegard of Bingen." *Vox Benedictina* 1 (1984): 257–63.

Kramnick, Isaac. "Children's Literature and Bourgeois Ideology: Observations on Culture and Industrial Capitalism in the Later Eighteenth Century." *Culture and Politics from Puritanism to the Enlightenment.* Ed. Perez Zagorin. Berkeley: U of California P, 1980.

Kristeva, Julia. *Powers of Horror: An Essay on Abjection.* Tr. L.S. Roudiez. New York: Columbia UP, 1982.

Laqueur, Thomas Walter. *Religion and Respectability: Sunday Schools and Working Class Culture 1780–1850*. New Haven: Yale UP, 1976.

Lead, Jane. *The Heavenly Cloud Now Breaking: The Lord Christ's Ascension-Ladder*. London: Printed for the Author, 1681.

———. *The Revelation of Revelations*. London: Printed and Sold by A. Sowle, 1683.

———. *The Enochian Walks with God, Found Out by a Spiritual Traveller, whose Face towards Mount-Sion Above was Set*. London: Printed and sold by D. Edwards, 1694.

———. *The Wonders of God's Creation Manifested in the Variety of Eight Worlds*. London: Printed and sold by T. Sowle, 1695.

———. *The Tree of Faith; or, the Tree of Life, Springing up in the Paradise of God; from which All the Wonders of the New Creation, in the Virgin Church of the Firstborn of Wisdom, must proceed*. London: Printed and sold by J. Bradford, 1696.

———. *A Fountain of Gardens Watered by the Rivers of Divine Pleasure*. London: Printed and sold by J. Bradford, 1696–1701.

———. *The Ascent to the Mount of Vision*. London: 1699.

———. *The Signs of the Times: Forerunning the Kingdom of Christ, and Evidencing When It Is Come*. London: J.P. Loutherbourg, 1699.

Leclerq, Jean. "Solitude and Solidarity: Medieval Women Recluses." *Medieval Religious Women: Peaceweavers*. Eds. L.T. Shank and J.A. Nicholls. Kalamazoo: Cistercian Publications, 1987. 67–84.

Lee, Sidney. ed. *Dictionary of National Biography*. London: Smith & Elder, 1909.

Lewis, Gertrude Jaron. "The Mystical *Jubilus:* An Example from Gertrud of Helfta (1256–1302)." *Vox Benedictina* 3 (1986): 237–47.

———. "The Mystical *Jubilus* II: An Example from Mechthild of Magdeburg (1207/12–ca.1282)." *Vox Benedictina* 3 (1986): 327–37.

Lewis, Joan. *Ecstatic Religion: An Anthropological Study of Spirit Possession and Shamanism*. Middlesex: Penguin, 1971.

Loades, Ann. *Searching for Lost Coins: Explorations in Christian Feminism*. Allison Park: Pickwick Publications, 1988.

MacIntyre, Alasdair. *After Virtue: A Study in Moral Theory*. London: Duckworth, 1981.

Massey, Marilyn Chapin. "Religion, Gender, and Ideology: A Historical Exploration." *Journal of Religion*. 67 (1987): 151–63.

Matter, E. Ann. " 'My Sister, My Spouse': Woman-Identified

Women in Medieval Christianity." *Journal of Feminist Studies in Religion* 2 (1986): 81–93.

McColley, Diane K. *Milton's Eve.* Urbana: U of Illinois P, 1983.

McFague, Sallie. *Metaphorical Theology: Models of God in Religious Language.* Philadelphia: Fortress, 1982.

———. *Models of God: Theology for an Ecological, Nuclear Age.* Philadelphia: Fortress, 1987

McNally, Robert E. *The Bible in the Early Middle Ages.* 1959. Reprinted Atlanta: Scholars Press, 1986.

Medcalf, Stephen. "Inner and Outer." *The Later Middle Ages.* Ed. S. Medcalf. London: Methuen, 1981. 108–71.

Meech, S.B. and H.E. Allen, ed. *The Book of Margery Kempe.* EETS #212. London: Oxford UP, 1940.

Meeks, Wayne A. "The Image of the Androgyne: Some Uses of a Symbol in Earliest Christianity." *History of Religions* 13 (1974): 165–203.

Menzies, Lucy, tr. *The Revelations of Mechthild of Magdeburg.* London: Longmans, Green, 1953.

Meyer, Ben F. *Critical Realism and the New Testament.* Allison Park: Pickwick Publications, 1989.

Meyers, Carol. *Discovering Eve: Ancient Israelite Women in Context.* New York: Oxford UP, 1988.

Miles, Margaret. *Image as Insight: Visual Understanding in Western Christianity and Secular Culture.* Boston: Beacon Press, 1985.

Miller, John W. "Depatriarchalizing God in Biblical Interpretation: A Critique." *Catholic Biblical Quarterly* 48 (1986): 609–16.

Millett, Bella, ed. *Hali Meidhad.* EETS #284. London: Oxford UP, 1982.

Mirandola, Pico della. "Oration on the Dignity of Man," in *The Renaissance Philosophy of Man,* ed. E. Cassirer, et al. Chicago: University of Chicago Press, 1948.

Mollenkott, Virginia R. "Some Implications of Milton's Androgynous Muse." *Bucknell Review* 24 (1978): 27–36.

———. *The Divine Feminine: The Biblical Imagery of God as Female.* New York: Crossroad, 1983.

More, Hannah. *Sacred Dramas.* London: William Milner, 1844.

———. *The Complete Works of Hannah More.* New York: Derby & Jackson, 1857.

Morgan, Robert and John Barton. *Biblical Interpretation.* Oxford: Oxford UP, 1988.

Mortimer, Favell Lee (Bevan). *Line Upon Line; or, A Second Series of*

the Earliest Instruction the Infant Mind is Capable of Receiving.
London: Hatchards, 1876.

———. *The Peep of Day; or, A Series of the Earliest Religious Instruction the Infant Mind is Capable of Receiving.* London: Hatchards, 1886.

Morton, Nelle. "Preaching the Word." *Sexist Religion and Women in the Church: No More Silence.* Ed. A.L. Hageman. New York: Association Press, 1974.

Mueller, Janel M. "Autobiography of a New 'Creature': Female Spirituality, Selfhood, and Authorship in *The Book of Margery Kempe.*" *Women in the Middle Ages and the Renaissance.* Ed. M.B. Rose. Syracuse: Syracuse UP, 1986. 155–72.

Mueller-Vollmer, Kurt, ed. *The Hermeneutics Reader: Texts of the German Tradition from the Enlightenment to the Present.* New York: Continuum, 1989.

Myers, Mitzi. "Impeccable Governesses, Rational Dames, and Moral Mothers: Mary Wollstonecraft and the Female Tradition in Georgian Children's Books." *Children's Literature* 14 (1986): 31–59.

Neel, Carol. "The Origin of the Beguines." *Signs* 14 (1989): 321–41.

Neumann, Erich. *The Great Mother: An Analysis of the Archetype.* Tr. R. Manheim. London: Routledge and KP, 1955.

Newman, Barbara. *Sister of Wisdom: St. Hildegard's Theology of the Feminine.* Berkeley: U of California P, 1987.

———, ed. *Saint Hildegard of Bingen Symphonia: A Critical Edition of the Symphonia armonie celestium revelationum.* Ithaca: Cornell UP, 1988.

Noffke, Suzanne, tr. *Catherine of Siena: The Dialogue.* New York: Paulist Press, 1980.

Nyquist, Mary. "The genesis of gendered subjectivity in the divorce tracts and in *Paradise Lost.*" *Re-membering Milton; Essays on the Texts and Traditions.* Ed. M. Nyquist and M. Ferguson. New York: Methuen, 1987. 99–127.

O., M.A. *The Glorious City: An Allegory for Children.* London: Joseph Masters, 1858.

Ochshorn, Judith. *The Female Experience and the Nature of the Divine.* Bloomington: Indiana UP, 1981.

Oesterle, Jean T., tr. *Aristotle: On Interpretation; Commentary by St. Thomas and Cajetan.* Milwaukee: Marquette UP, 1962.

Origen, *Origen:* First Principles, Book IV, trans. R.A. Greer. New York: Paulist Press, 1979.

Osiek, Carolyn. "The Feminist and the Bible: Hermeneutical Alternatives." *Feminist Perspectives on Biblical Scholarship.* Ed. A.Y. Collins. Chico: Scholars Press, 1985. 93–106.

———. "The New Handmaid: The Bible and the Social Sciences." *Theological Studies* 50 (1989): 260–78.

Otto, Rudolph. *The Idea of the Holy: An Inquiry into the Non-Rational Factor in the Idea of the Divine and Its Relation to the Rational.* Trans. J.W. Harvey. London: Oxford UP, 1925.

Otwell, John H. *And Sarah Laughed: The Status of Woman in the Old Testament.* Philadelphia: Westminster, 1977.

Pagels, Elaine. *The Gnostic Gospels.* New York: Random House, 1979.

———. *Adam, Eve and the Serpent.* New York: Random House, 1988.

Patai, Raphael. *The Hebrew Goddess.* New York: KTAV, 1767.

Peers, E. Allison, trans. *The Complete Works of Saint Teresa of Jesus.* London: Sheed & Ward, 1944–46.

Penny, A.J. *Studies in Jacob Boehme.* London: John Watkins, 1912.

Perkins, Pheme. *The Gnostic Dialogue: The Early Church and the Crisis of Gnosticism.* New York: Paulist Press, 1980.

Petroff, Elizabeth Alvida, ed. *Medieval Women's Visionary Literature.* New York: Oxford UP, 1986.

Pickering, Samuel F. *John Locke and Children's Books in Eighteenth-Century England.* Knoxville: U of Tennessee P, 1981.

Pinchbeck, Ivy and Margaret Hewitt. *Children in English Society.* London: Routledge and KP, 1969.

Pisan, Christine de. *Le Livre de la Mutacion de Fortune, publié d'après les manuscrits par Suzanne Solente.* Tome I. Paris: Editions A. and J. Picard, 1959.

———. *The Book of the City of Ladies.* Trans. E.J. Richards. New York: Persea, 1982.

———. *The Treasure of the City of Ladies.* Trans. S. Lawson. Middlesex: Penguin, 1985.

Plumb, J.H. "The New World of Children in Eighteenth-Century England." *Past and Present* 67 (1975): 64–95.

Prickett, Stephen. *Words and the Word: Language, Poetics and Biblical Interpretation.* Cambridge: Cambridge UP, 1986.

Proctor-Smith, Marjorie. "Liturgical Anamnesis and Women's Memory: 'Something Missing.' " *Worship* 61 (1987): 405–24.

Puttenham, George. *The Arte of English Poesie.* Eds. G.D. Willcock and A. Walker. Cambridge: Cambridge UP, 1936.

Radzinowicz, Mary Ann. "How and Why the Literary Establish-

ment Caught Up with the Bible: Instancing the Book of Job."
Christianity and Literature 39 (1989): 77–89.

Renna, Thomas. "Virginity in the *Life* of Christina of Markyate and Aeldred of Rievaulx's *Rule.*" *American Benedictine Review* 36 (1985): 79–92.

Ricoeur, Paul. "Philosophical Hermeneutics and Theological Hermeneutics." *Studies in Religion/ Sciences Religieuses* 5 (1975): 14–33.

———. "Biblical Hermeneutics." *Semeia* 4 (1975): 36–50.

———. *Essays on Biblical Interpretation.* Ed. Lewis S. Mudge. Philadelphia: Fortress, 1980.

Rosman, Doreen. *Evangelicals and Culture.* London: Croom Helm, 1984.

Ruether, Rosemary Radford, ed. *Religion and Sexism: Images of Women in the Jewish and Christian Traditions.* New York: Simon and Schuster, 1974.

———. "Review of *Bread Not Stone.*" *Journal of the American Academy of Religion* 54 (1986): 141–43.

Ruether, R. R. and E. McLaughlin, eds. *Women of Spirit: Female Leadership in the Jewish and Christian Traditions.* New York: Simon and Schuster, 1979.

Russell, Letty, ed. *Feminist Interpretation of the Bible.* Philadelphia: Westminster, 1985.

St. John, Christopher, tr. *The Plays of Roswitha.* London: Chatto & Windus, 1923.

Schleiermacher, Friedrich. *Hermeneutics: The Handwritten Manuscripts.* Tr. J. Duke and J. Forstman. Missoula: Scholars Press, 1977.

Schneiders, Sandra. *Women and the Word: The Gender of God in the New Testament and the Spirituality of Women.* New York: Paulist Press, 1986.

Scholem, Gershom. *Major Trends in Jewish Mysticism.* New York: Schocken, 1969.

Schreck, Nancy and Maureen Leech, eds. *Psalms Anew: In Inclusive Language.* Winona: St. Mary's Press, 1986.

Schreiner, Olive. *The Story of an African Farm.* New York: Rand, McNally, 1883.

Scrope, Stephen, tr. *The Epistle of Othea to Hector or The Boke of Knyghthode.* London: J.B. Nichols and Sons, 1904.

Setel, Drorah. "Feminist Insights and the Question of Method." *Feminist Perspectives on Biblical Scholarship.* Ed. A.Y. Collins. Chico: Scholars Press, 1985. 35–42.

Shechter, Patricia, et al. "A Vision of Feminist Religious Scholarship." *Journal of Feminist Studies in Religion* 3 (1987): 91–111.

Sherwood, Mrs. (Mary Martha Butt). *The History of Little Henry and His Bearer.* Second Edition. Wellington: F. Houlston & Son, 1815.

———. *The Infant's Progress From the Valley of Destruction to Everlasting Glory.* Wellington: F. Houlston & Son, 1825.

Simpson, Evelyn M., ed. *John Donne's Sermons on the Psalms and Gospels.* Berkeley: U of California P, 1963.

Smalley, Beryl. *The Study of the Bible in the Middle Ages.* Third Edition. Oxford: Blackwell, 1983.

Smith, Catherine F. "Jane Lead: The Feminist Mind and Art of a Seventeenth-Century Protestant Mystic." *Women of Spirit.* Ed. R.R. Ruether. New York: Simon & Schuster, 1979. 184–203.

———. "Jane Lead: Mysticism and the Woman Cloathed with the Sun." *Shakespeare's Sisters: Feminist Essays on Women Poets.* Eds. S.M. Gilbert and S. Gubar. Bloomington: Indiana UP, 1979. 3–18.

Sticca, Sandro. "Hrotsvitha's *Dulcitius* and Christian Symbolism." *Medieval Studies* 32 (1970): 108–27.

Stone, Merlin. *The Paradise Papers: The Suppression of Women's Rites.* London: Virago, 1976.

Stretton, Hesba. *Jessica's First Prayer.* London: R.T.S., 1867.

———. *Pilgrim Street: A Story of Manchester Life.* London: R.T.S., 1870.

———. *Little Meg's Children.* 1868. London: R.T.S., 1875.

———. *Alone in London.* London: R.T.S., 1880.

Summerfield, Geoffrey. *Fantasy and Reason: Children's Literature in the Eighteenth Century.* Athens: U of Georgia P, 1984.

Talbott, James. *The Christian School-Master.* A New Edition. 1707. London: F.C. & J. Rivington, 1811.

Taves, Ann. "Mothers and Children and the Legacy of Mid-nineteenth-century American Christianity." *Journal of Religion* 67 (1987): 203–19.

Taylor, Barbara. *Eve and the New Jerusalem: Socialism and Feminism in the Nineteenth Century.* London: Virago, 1983.

Taylor, Charles. *Sources of the Self: The Making of the Modern Identity.* Cambridge: Harvard UP, 1989.

Tennis, Diane. *Is God the Only Reliable Father?* Philadelphia: Westminster, 1985.

Thune, Nils. *The Behmenists and the Philadelphians: A Contribution to* the Study of English Mysticism in the Seventeenth and Eighteenth Centuries. Uppsala: Almquist & Wiksells Boktryckeri, 1948.

Tolbert, Mary Ann. "Defining the Problem: The Bible and Feminist Hermeneutics," Semeia 28 (1983): 113–126.

Toole, John Kennedy. A Confederacy of Dunces. New York: Grove, 1980.

Tracy, David. The Analogical Imagination: Christian Theology and the Culture of Pluralism. New York: Crossroad, 1981.

Trapnel, Anna. The Cry of the Stone or a Relation of Something Spoken in Whitehall, by Anna Trapnel, being in the Visions of God. London, 1654.

Trible, Phyllis. "Depatriarchalism in Biblical Interpretation." Journal of American Academy of Religion 41 (1973): 30–40.

———. "The Gift of a Poem: A Rhetorical Study of Jeremiah 31:15–22." Andover Newton Quarterly 17 (1977): 271–80.

———. God and the Rhetoric of Sexuality. Philadelphia: Fortress Press, 1978.

———. Texts of Terror; Literary Feminist Readings of Biblical Narratives. Philadelphia: Fortress Press, 1984.

———. "Five Loaves and Two Fishes: Feminist Hermeneutics and Biblical Theology." Theological Studies 50 (1989): 279–95.

Trimmer, Mrs. (Sarah). The Charity School Spelling Book. Fifth Edition. London: F. & C. Rivington, 1799.

———. A Comparative View of the New Plan of Education Promulgated by Mr. Joseph Lancaster. London: F., C. and J. Rivington, 1805.

———. Essay on Christian Education. The Guardian of Education. 5 vols. London: J. Hatchard, 1802–1806.

Tucker, Charlotte (A.L.O.E.). The Lake of the Woods: A Tale Illustrative of the Twelfth Chapter of Romans. London: Gall & Inglis, 1867.

———. Life in the White Bear's Den. A Tale of Labrador. London: Gall & Inglis, 1884.

———. The Crown of Success; or, Four Heads to Furnish. 1859. London: T. Nelson, 1886.

Turner, Victor. Dramas, Fields, and Metaphors: Symbolic Action in Human Society. Ithaca: Cornell UP, 1974.

Walsh, David. The Mysticism of Innerworldly Fulfillment; A Study of Jacob Boehme. Gainesville: Florida UP, 1983.

Warner, Marina. Alone of All Her Sex: The Myth and Cult of the Virgin Mary. London: Weidenfeld & Nicolson, 1976.

———. Monuments and Maidens: The Allegory of the Female Form. New York: Atheneum, 1985.

Warner, Sylvia Townsend. *The Corner That Held Them*. London: Chatto & Windus, 1948.

Watley, William, ed. *The Word and Words: Beyond Gender in Theological and Liturgical Language*. Princeton: Women's Task Force Worship Commission, 1983.

Wegner, Judith Romney. *Chattel or Person? The Status of Women in the Mishnah*. New York: Oxford University Press, 1988.

Wehr, Demaris. *Jung and Feminism: Liberating Archetypes*. London: Routledge, 1988.

Weinstein, Donald and Rudolph Bell. *Saints and Society: The Two Worlds of Western Christendom 1100–1700*. Chicago: U of Chicago P, 1982.

White, Hayden. "The Politics of Historical Interpretation: Discipline and De-Sublimation." *Critical Inquiry* 8 (1982): 113–137.

White, Thomas. *A Little Book for Little Children. Wherein are set down several Directions for Little Children; and several remarkable Stories both Ancient and Modern of Little Children, Divers whereof are of those who are lately deceased*. London: Joseph Cranford, 1660.

Willard, Charity Cannon. *Christine de Pizan: Her Life and Works*. New York: Persea, 1984.

Wilson, Katherina M., ed. *Medieval Women Writers*. Athens: U of Georgia P, 1984.

———. "Antonomasia as a Means of Character-Definition in the Works of Hrotsvit of Gandersheim." *Rhetorica* 2 (1984): 45–53.

———. "Hrotsvit and the Tube: John Kennedy Toole and the Problem of Bad TV Programming." *Germanic Notes* 15 (1984): 4–5.

———, tr. *The Dramas of Hrotsvit of Gandersheim*. Saskatoon: Matrologia Latina, 1985.

———. "*Figmenta vs. Veritas:* Dame Alice and the Medieval Literary Depiction of Women by Women." *Tulsa Studies in Women's Literature* 4 (1985): 17–32.

———. "Hrotsvit and the *Artes:* Learning *Ad Usum Meliorem*." *The Worlds of Medieval Women, Creativity, Influence and Imagination*. Eds. C. Berman, C. Connell, J. Rothchild. Morgantown: West Virginia UP, 1985.

———. "Hrotsvit's *Abraham:* A Lesson in Etymology." *Germanic Notes* 16 (1985): 2–4.

———, ed. *Women Writers of the Renaissance and Reformation*. Athens: U of Georgia P, 1987.

———. *Hrotsvit of Gandersheim: The Ethics of Authorial Stance*. Leiden: E.J. Brill, 1988.

Windeatt, B.A., tr. *The Book of Margery Kempe.* Middlesex: Penguin, 1985.

Wolters, Clifton, trans. *The Cloud of Unknowing.* Middlesex: Penguin, 1961.

Young, Karl. *Drama of the Medieval Church.* Oxford: Clarendon, 1933.

Zeydel, Edwin. "Were Hrotsvitha's Dramas Performed During Her Lifetime?" *Speculum* 20 (1943): 443–56.

————. "A Note on Hrotsvit's Aversion to Synalepha." *PQ* 23 (1944): 379–81.

————. "On the Two Minor Poems in the Hrotsvitha Codex." *MLN* 60 (1945): 373–76.

————. "The Reception of Hrotsvitha by the German Humanists after 1493." *JEGP* 44 (1945): 443–56.

————. " 'Ego Clamor Validus'—Hrotsvitha." *MLN* 64 (1946): 281–83.

————. "The Authenticity of Hrotsvitha's Works." *MLN* 69 (1946): 50–55.

Index

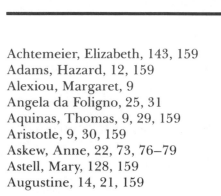

Index of Biblical References